The
Scots
and their
Oats

The Scots and their Oats

Wallace Lockhart

Birlinn

Published in Great Britain, 1997, from a first edition,
revised and updated, of *The Scot and His Oats*,
Birlinn Limited
14 High Street
Edinburgh EH1 1TE

British Library Cataloguing-in-Publication Data
A Catalogue record of this book is available
from the British Library.

ISBN 1 874744 80 7

Designed and typeset in 10.5/12pt Berkeley
by Janet Watson

Made and printed in Finland by
Werner Söderström OY

Contents

Preface to the Second Edition

During the re-writing and extending of this second edition, first published as *The Scot and His Oats* in 1983 by Luath Press, I have taken the opportunity to make contact again with old friends in the world of 'Oats' and establish new links with those engaged in some facet of work associated with the crop and its products. To them all, I record my thanks for the help so willingly given.

In particular I would express quite inadequate thanks to Tom Rogers of Cupar and the Aberfeldy Water Mill and Colin Brown and Kate Wellwood of Scotts Porage Oats. Ian Millar of Hogarth's of Kelso reminded me of the joys of country milling, while Gavin Love of Simmers expanded my horizons. James Walker of 'Walkers of Aberlour', as in the past, came to my aid and the world of the mealie pudding was explained to me by W.H. Robertson of Edinburgh. My thanks also go to Peter Martin of the Economics and Statistics Unit of the Scottish Office who supplied me with much interesting information.

Some of the pictures from the first edition have been retained. Additional material has been obtained from our National Museum, which I acknowledge with thanks.

Kerr's Music of Glasgow have given me permission to quote from 'McGinty's Meal and Ale' and I am extremely grateful to the family of the late Charles Murray for allowing me to quote 'The Hint O' Hairst' and 'The Miller Explains'.

Finally, for the giving of encouragement and all her toil, I am immeasurably indebted to my wife.

Introduction

For me, I can be weel content,
To eat my bannock on the bent,
And kitchen't wi' fresh air;
O' lang kail I can mak a feast,
And cantily haud up my crest
And laugh at dishes rare.

'The Poet's Wish – An Ode', Allan Ramsay, 1686-1758

As a boy, I hated porridge. The grey, bubbling mass in the black pot did not hold for me the relish it held for others. Worse than that, it seemed to me, in my little world, that everything centred around the making and eating of it. The Howe of Strathmore was filled with field upon field of oats, all apparently destined to finish up in the breakfast bowls of small boys. How that gently swaying, delicate, golden crop which so tingled the senses could bring such misery in its train was something my mind could not absorb. But I was the odd-man-out. My friends loved their porridge and oatmeal in all its forms. As we cooked our trout, taken from the burns in the Angus glens, the fish were invisible under their smothering of oatmeal. My pride would not let me complain, and I joined in the acclaim that we were feeding like kings.

The corn fields at harvest-time were sheer bliss. The stubble crunched under our feet as we ran round the stooks and if a mass of bites was the price to pay for being able to hide under the sheaves while stalking a courting couple, it was of little importance.

The passing years brought greater knowledge of the oat crop. One learned to identify the different varieties by rubbing out a few grains in the hands: 'Marvellous' with its green tip, tubby 'Onward' and 'Golden Rain' with its distinctive colour. Wild oats were seldom seen, but when they were noticed standing proud of the crop they were ruthlessly rogued out. Scots Seed Oats were famous and no contamination was permissible. Occasionally the Potato Oat was encountered. Legend has it that this oat was discovered growing in a field of potatoes around the year 1800 and, because of its plumpness, it was kept for seed and multiplied. Its original habitat was the subject of much correspondence to farming papers in the early nineteenth century, claims being made for Turkey and South America as well as Essex and Cumberland. What is certain is that it was superior to any other oat at the time of its introduction, and that in the Fiars' Courts (referred to later on in the book), it was for many years separately priced.

Army service followed school, and this intervention provided an escape from porridge. As everyone knows, the Scot makes porridge with salt; the cooks in my regiment being English, they made it with sugar. Thus, proclaiming that I would not offend my nationality, I was able to avoid the fearsome stuff with dignity – even I fear, with a touch of rudeness. 'Haggis' might have been my soldiering nickname, but eat sweetened porridge I would not.

Maturity (or was it army sustenance?) civilised my palate, and when I entered the grain trade I found I could nibble away at the freshly ground oatmeal issuing from the mill with some enjoyment. That was some kind of bonus as I was discovering that the expression 'going through the mill' was no empty phrase. The range of skills to be learned, seemed never-ending and I still wonder at the physical demands that were placed on us. A later sojourn in Canada introduced me to the coating of porridge with maple syrup and the much more acceptable honey. But it was the waving crops of oats in British Columbia and the

Prairie Provinces which confirmed my affection for the crop, although their yields and plumpness of grain were not on a par with Scottish crops. Every year, at the Winter Agricultural Fair held in Toronto, a competition was held to find the world's best sample of oats, and every year, it seemed, the challenge was won by oats from a Scottish farm. I returned to this country, a dedicated oatmeal addict.

The nationalism of the Scot expands when he leaves his native land. He needs no lessons in propaganda. Hogmanay, St Andrew's night, Burns' Suppers, ensure the world knows when the Scots are around. And the menus, with their proliferation of haggis, oatcakes, Athole Brose and crannachan remind three thousand million people of the staple foods of a nation. The wonder of it is that the Scot is not only tolerated, but encouraged and emulated in his vauntings. No other race would get away with it. Wilfred Taylor, that great doyen of Scottish journalists of yesteryear, in his book *Scot Free* (1953), recounts the story of the Scot who arrived in some far-off jungle-land to discover, to his horror, that St Andrew's day had never been celebrated in the locality. He immediately started issuing invitations. Out of a total neighbouring population of 360 Europeans, 250 attended. An Englishman who had accepted his invitation was so stung that he set about arranging a St George's day function the following year. It was attended by seven people, all of them Southrons. And Wilfred Taylor continues:

> So resounding has been the success of St Andrew's nights in places like Singapore and Buenos Aires that in recent years even Scots at home have started to celebrate the occasion. Since few of the homeland Scots have any clear idea of who the fisherman saint was or what he stood for those festivals have been rather tame and obviously activated by the Scottish Office, an institution with a boundless enthusiasm for temperate patriotism.
>
> 'Scot Free', Wilfred Taylor, 1953

Hugh MacDiarmid, of course, took a more trenchant view

of such Scottish activities, and in 'A Drunk Man Looks At The Thistle', rasps out:

> *You canna gang to a Burns supper even*
> *Wi'oot some wizened scrint o' a knock-knee*
> *Chinee turns roon to say, 'Him Haggis – velly goot!'*
> *and ten to wan the piper is a Cockney.*

Some exiles' celebrations of course, are more noted for their enthusiasm than their authenticity. Arriving to speak at a St Andrew's night dinner in Yorkshire some years ago, I was handed a large glass of Athole Brose by my host, who expressed the hope that it would get me into the right frame of mind. It was an ambiguous invitation. The Brose had the consistency of putty.

Today, porridge and bannocks and all our other oatmeal friends are with us as they were yesteryear. Yet I wonder how many Scots realise their dependency on oats apart from its traditional uses. As he and she munch their Hobnob with their coffee or pour yoghurt over their muesli, do they realise their basic enjoyment is coming from the flaked oat content? Indeed the present palate desire is for a good bite of oats and millers and bakers are responding by producing 'jumbo' flakes made from the whole groat rather than the divided groat in the form of pinhead oatmeal.

In this little book I have tried to trace the journey of the oat crop; not only from field to factory but over the centuries as an integral part of Scottish life. Such a historical and social study, light-hearted as it may be, inevitably shows just how much the Scots owe to their oats. I hope you will enjoy the journey with me.

Peace to the husbandman and a' his tribe,
Whase care fells a' our wants frae year to year!
Lang may his sock and cou'ter turn the glybe,
And banks o' corn bend down wi' laded ear!
May Scotia's simmers ay look gay and green;
Her yellow har'sts frae scowry blasts decreed!
May a' her tenants sit fu' snug and bien,
Frae the hard grip o' ails, and poortith freed;
And a lang lasting train o' peacefu' hours succeed!

'The Farmers Ingle', Robert Fergusson, 1750-1774

1
The Oat Crop

The yellow corn waves in the field,
The merry hairst's begun;
And steel-plate sickles, sharp and keen,
Are glintin' in the sun,
While strappin' lads, and lassies braw,
A' kiltit to the knee,
Bring to my mind a hairst langsyne,
When Robin shuire wi' me.

'Hairst', James Thomson, 1827-1888

From at least the fifteenth century poets and chroniclers have regularly told of the importance of the oat crop in Scotland. It is perfectly understandable; seldom has a crop been so associated with a people and their way of life. For hundreds of years, oats, in one form or another, served as a staple diet of the population. Together with its straw, the oat helped to fatten the famous black cattle, while the straw on its own was plaited into curtains for doors and used for paper-making. Oatmeal had value as a currency in the payment for rent or wages or to form part of a dowry. Oat poultices were used to draw poisons from the body, and the harvesting of the crop provided themes for many songs, especially in later years for the great bothy ballads of the north-east.

Oats, of course, with their high-energy value, are the great food for horses. As every Scottish schoolboy used to know, Dr Johnson, the eminent lexicographer, commented

1

that the Scots lived on the food which in England was given to horses, and indeed went so far as to give such a definition in his first dictionary. Perhaps it was the riposte from Lord Elibank: 'And where will you get such men and such horses?' that led to its later suppression.

Fergusson, that great vernacular poet and forerunner of Burns, very obviously was not impressed by Johnson's remark, and in his poem describing the treat given to the eminent literary figure by the professors of St Andrews' University, was determined to set the record straight:

> *Mind ye what Sam, the lying loun,*
> *Has in his Dictionare laid down?*
> *That aits, in England, are a feast*
> *To cow and horse, and sicken beast;*
> *While in Scots ground this growth was common*
> *To gust the gab o' man and woman.*
> *Tak tent, ye Regents! then, and hear*
> *My list o' gudely hameil gear,*
> *Sic as hae aften rax'd the wame*
> *O' blyther fallows miny time:*
> *Mair hardy, souple, steeve and swank,*
> *Than ever stood on Sammy's shank.*
>
> 'Lines to the Principal and Professors of the University of
> St Andrews on their Superb Treat to Dr Samual Johnson',
> Robert Fergusson, 1750-1774

We Scots seem to be particularly unforgiving about Dr Johnson's remark. Even at the turn of this century, Robert Ford could relate, with obvious pleasure, in *Thistledown*, an occasion when the Doctor got paid back in his own coin:

> *Soon after his return from Scotland to London, a Scotch lady resident in the capital invited him to dinner, and in compliment to her distinguished guest ordered a dish of hotch-potch. When the great man had tasted it, she asked him if it was good, to which he replied, with his usual gruffness, 'Very good for hogs, I believe!'*
>
> *'Then, pray,' said the lady, 'let me help you to a little more;' and she did.*

2

There is, however, on record one event which acknowledges the importance of the oat being an acceptable food for both man and horse. During the Boer War, when the beleaguered garrison of Mafeking was virtually out of provisions, it was able to keep itself alive by making a gruel from the scrapings of the horse-feed boxes.

The oat is a very old cereal crop. Believed to have originated in Asia, probably as a deviant of oat-grass, it spread westwards and was known on the European Continent more than two thousand years ago. Hippocrates (fifth century BC) refers to the crop and Virgil (first century BC) was apparently enough of a farmer to complain that oats had the ability to choke out barley; and to the Greeks goes the honour of first recognising the value of a porridge made from oats.

Although the oat can be grown under widely varying conditions of soil and climate, it is at its best where the weather is cool and early summer rainfall provides the conditions for the kernel to fill out with slow maturity. Scotland provides such conditions and the crop's journey north was therefore assured. With natural selection being aided by the husbandman's selection of the best plants for seed, yields of grain increased and the crop began to take an increasingly important place in the economy. By the thirteenth century it was established as a popular food crop, sharing a place with barley. Improvements to the crop continued to be made, and by the early 1600s, oats were classified in the Fiars' Courts, where prices were agreed for oats and oatmeal. Not a great deal of information is available about the origin of Fiars' Courts, but their general function was the relating of the rent, and in some cases the feu duty, to be paid by the tenant to the value of the crops produced on the farm. The values arrived at in these courts served as a rule for ascertaining the prices of grain in all contracts where they were not fixed by the parties, and in many sales it was agreed to accept the rates fixed by the fiars. Until the Church of Scotland rationalised the stipends paid to ministers, it was customary to base the stipend on the value of the crops grown in the parish, using the Fiars' Courts' prices. Writing last century, a Mr Barclay, the sheriff-substitute of Perthshire gave an account of the process as practised in that county:

> *The Fiars' Court is held on the last Friday of February or the first Friday of March. The jury consists of eight heritors [property owners], a few farmers and some neutral parties, especially one or two able to check the calculations. Some years ago it was arranged to take no juror who either paid or received rents according to the fiars; but this greatly limited the choice, and was complained of, and abandoned. All considerable dealers in Perthshire victual, whether resident in Perthshire or elsewhere, are uniformly summoned, and in addition every person whose name is given in by whatever person interested.*

> Chambers' Encyclopaedia, 1906

It must not be thought that the Fiars' Courts solved all problems. A free market was still in existence and as John Galt, writing in the early nineteenth century would relate in *The Provost*, the public responds unkindly when it feels it is being over-charged:

> *Some of the farmers were loading their carts to go home, when the schools skailed, and all the weans came shouting to the market. Still nothing happened, till tinkler Jean, a randy that had been with the army at the siege of Gibraltar, and, for all I ken, in the Americas, if no in the Indies likewise; she came with her meal-basin in her hand, swearing like a trooper that if she didna get it filled with meal at fifteen pence a peck, (the farmers demanded sixteen) she would have the fu'o't of their heart's blood: and the mob of thoughtless weans and idle fellows, with shouts and yells, encouraged Jean and egged her on to a catastrophe. The corruption of the farmers was thus raised and a rash young lad, in an unguarded moment, lifted his hand and struck her. He himself swore an affidavit that he gave her only a ding*

4

*out of his way; but be this as it may, at him rushed Jean
with open mouth and broke her timber meal-basin on
his head, as if it had been an egg-shell.*

By the eighteenth century, white, black and grey oats were
recognised as distinctive and the naming of strains within
these categories was soon to follow. As the grain trade
developed in the nineteenth century, seed from various
Continental varieties was imported for crossing with indige-
nous strains, leading in turn to the breeding and growing of
higher yielding strains. The selection of seed became more
scientific, and leading farmers, seed merchants and the
Colleges of Agriculture began to establish field trials to
ascertain the best and most appropriate varieties of oats
to grow in different parts of the country. All this led to
the magnificent crops of oats seen this century. Anyone
suggesting to a farmer of yesteryear that three tons to the
acre crop would become commonplace would have been
considered weak in the head.

It had long been considered that seed produced in the
harsher climate of the northern parts of the United
Kingdom was healthier, plumper and higher yielding than
that produced in more southern climes. This was the basis
on which was established the seed export trade to England
which, even to the middle of this century, saw thousands
of tons of seed oats every year make the journey south by
road or rail. For a while too, a modest export trade was
carried on with some southern African countries. At one
time, also, race-horse owners were avid buyers of black
oats, believing them to give their steeds extra pace, but
that specialist trade has decreased, if not disappeared
altogether. Australian oats are currently said to be the
secret weapon for speed.

As the oat crop in Scotland grew in popularity, so
too did the sophistication of the tools and equipment
associated with it. The jump from the picking of the ears
by hand to the introduction of the sickle was indeed a
gigantic technological advance. The sickle, which frequently had a toothed cutting edge, allowed a man, or just

as often a woman, to cut a good quarter of an acre of oats in a day. It is strange that the scythe, which had been known in Roman times, and was presumably used for mowing grass, took such a long time to be employed in the harvesting of grain crops. A factor might be that, because the oat harvest was later in the year in the Middle Ages than it is nowadays with earlier-ripening varieties of oats, the crop would have been flattened by the weather and thus difficult to scythe. Other factors against the scythe were its greater need for level ground than the sickle, a greater reputation for shaking out too much grain, and, of course, it was a man's rather than a woman's instrument needing a greater strength and longer arms to be worked effectively. So a division of labour entered the harvest scene, the most competent men with the scythe cutting the corn, the women gathering and making the bands for the sheaves and the other men binding and stooking the sheaves. Willie Scott, born in Aberdeenshire in 1785, had no difficulty in describing the operation in song:

> O' a' the seasons o' the year
> When we maun work the sairest,
> The harvest is the only time,
> And yet it is the fairest.
> We rise as seen at morning licht,
> Nae craters can be blither:
> We buckle on oor finger-steels,
> And follow oot the scyther.
>
> I'll gie ye bands that winna slip,
> I'll pleat them weel and thraw them;
> I'm sure they winna tine the grip,
> Hooever weel ye draw them.
> I'll lay my leg oot owre the sheaf,
> And draw the band sae handy,
> Wi' ilka strae as straucht's a rash,
> And that'll be the dandy.

'Johnnie Sangster', Willie Scott, c.1800

The first scythes to be used on a large scale had a cradle arrangement fitted to them which allowed the crop to be set out in more regular swathes and the rate of cutting per man rose to over an acre a day.

Up to the beginning of the nineteenth century, gangs of blue-bonneted Highland men and Highland lasses moved to the Lowlands every year to take part in the harvest, gradually working their way north again as the harvest progressed. The morals of these Highland workers were of considerable concern to the Church, the Sabbath frequently not being strictly observed by them and the young girls spending their money unwisely on fripperies. Where large gangs were employed, and these gangs could be of sixty or more in strength, the farmer might also engage a piper as an inducement to greater productivity.

The early nineteenth century saw the harvesting work being increasingly taken over by Irish workers. *The Glasgow Chronicle* of 17 August 1824 records that the Irish were more prominent than Highlanders at the local shearers' market. With cheap boat fares working to their advantage, it is said forty thousand seasonal workers were arriving by the middle of the century. But even last century, employment and high technology were to be ill-at-ease in each other's company. The introduction of the reaper reduced the need for massive harvesting gangs.

But the nostalgic link with these past harvesting days is strong:

Whan the auld fowk sit quaiet at the reet o' a stook,
I' the sunlicht their washt een blinterin and blinkin,
Fowk scythin, or bin'in, or shearin wi' heuk
Carena a strae what the auld fowk are thinkin.
'What the Auld Fowk are Thinkin', George Macdonald, 1824-1905

Credit for inventing the first really workable reaper is normally given to the Reverend Patrick Bell of Carmyllie in Angus. The reaper cut the stalks and laid them in a row for tying. People had struggled hard to find a way to harvest cereals in something akin to comfort. Pliny the

Elder, who was born in the first century, came across a reaping machine in Gaul and records:

> *In the extensive fields in the lowlands of Gaul vans of a large size, with projecting teeth on the edge, are driven on two wheels through the standing corn by an ox yoked in a reverse position. In this manner the ears are torn off, and fall into the van.*

Chambers' Encylopaedia, 1906

Many of the early attempts to design a reaper involved the use of horses 'pushing' rather than 'pulling' a vehicle and it was not until the idea of side delivery was pursued that the normal horse position was achieved. But Bell's invention, although widely acclaimed, was not taken up at speed by Scottish farmers. Drainage and the levelling of ground had first to be tackled before the benefits of the reaper could be enjoyed.

In 1878, McCormack in America produced the string-tying self binder, which was shortly afterwards manufactured in Scotland by T.S. Bisset and Son of Blairgowrie. The binder was to become the epitome of the harvest to following generations. A wonderfully intricate machine (it boasted thirty grease nipples), drawn by a pair of heavy work-horses, it not only cut the crop in five- or six-foot swathes but tied the sheaves with twine before throwing them to the side in rows as it moved around the field. Many binders were to figure in harvest-scene photographs and paintings.

The tied sheaves from the binder would be set against each other in stooks of six to ten, or even more sheaves, facing north and south so that both sides would get their share of sunlight for drying and ripening. Wind or heavy rain would often cause the stooks to topple; the straightening of sodden stooks of an unbelievable weight was a hard and unpopular task, especially if they contained nettles or thistles. Again, if the stooks were taking a long time to dry and a new grass crop was shooting up, the stooks would have to be moved to avoid smothering the young grass. Then, when eventually considered fit for stacking, they would be taken to the stackyard.

The stackyard was normally situated near the barn; a windy spot had advantages as it allowed the drying out of the grain to continue. When horses were used to do this 'leading', a 'kepper' would be fitted into the animals' mouths to prevent them from eating the sheaves.

The stack was normally built around a wooden tripod and on a raised floor of overlapping stones to encourage circulation of air and make it more difficult for rats and mice to take up residence. Building a stack was skilled work, normally done by the grieve. It was important that each layer of sheaves was built with the grain-end slightly higher than the butt-end to ensure that rain would run off and not penetrate the stack encouraging heating and moulding. When a stack showed signs of heating it had to be taken apart and the sheaves cooled down before re-building, a humiliating experience for the man who had built the first stack. To save face it was customary to provide a sound reason for the dismantling; 'the grieve lost his watch in the stack and we're looking for it' was an acknowledged standby excuse.

A well-built stack was a handsome edifice. Frequently a good twenty feet in height, the last few feet were tapered and the final operation was to thatch the stack, frequently with rushes, to make it waterproof and rope it down to withstand heavy winds. Then at the top could often be seen an example of one of the most delightful of country crafts, 'the corn dolly'.

It must be remembered that in the days before the advent of the combine harvester, the harvesting of crops involved long hours of toil spread over many weeks. So the end of harvest was an occasion for great satisfaction and rejoicing and was marked by a festivity known as a 'Kirn' or a 'Meal and Ale' or a 'Muckle Supper'. In the north-east, the term 'Meal and Ale' was used to describe the drink provided as well as the occasion itself; and a potent mixture it was too, consisting of whisky, ale, sugar and oatmeal. Stories abound about the happenings at 'Meal and Ales' and have been passed down the generations, particularly in bothy ballads. Fiddles and melodeons would play; there would be drinking, dancing and singing, leading to wilder activities such as riding pigs bare-back round the steading. Sadly, such 'Kirns' were not always celebrated, especially in the crofting lands in the north-west of Scotland. There the crops, thin at any time because of the poor soil, would often stand in the stooks for months, battered by rain and wind, the grain sprouting on the stalk, losing its feeding value, depriving families of their winter sustenance. For them there would be no such songs as:

> They had spurtles, they had tattie chappers, faith they
> werena' jokin',
> And they swore they'd gar the pig claw whaur he was
> never yokin',
> But by this time the lad was fou' and didna care a dockin'
> At McGinty's Meal and Ale whaur the pig ga'ed on the
> spree.
> Oh! there's eelie pigs an' jeelie pigs an' pigs for haudin'
> butter,
> Aye but this pig was greetin' fou and rowin' in the gutter,
> Till McGinty and his foreman trailed him oot upon a
> shutter,
> Frae McGinty's Meal and Ale whaur the pig ga'ed on the
> spree.

'McGinty's Meal and Ale', George Bruce Thomson, 1950

Rituals also centred round the last sheaf to be cut. It might be given to the best milk cow in the byre, or shared out amongst the beasts at Christmas, or given to the first horse to start the next year's cultivation. Harvest then, saw the end of the farming year, mentally, if not physically a time for rest, a time to welcome words such as Hew Ainslie's:

> It's dowie in the hint o' hairst,
> At the wa'gang o' the swallow,
> When the wind grows cauld, and the burns grow bauld,
> An' the wuds are hingin' yellow.

'Dowie in One Hind O Mause', Hew Ainslie, 1792-1877

The oats in the stackyard would be threshed out through the year according to need; the grain to bring in money, being sold for milling or feeding or going for seed, the straw to provide fodder for the beasts in the cattle courts or byre, or, more reluctantly, for bedding.

The first ways of separating the grain from the straw were extremely primitive and involved hand-rubbing the heads or allowing oxen to tread the sheaves. An improvement on this latter approach, practised by the ancient Egyptians and the Israelites, was the threshing sledge, a frame mounted on rollers which was pulled over the sheaves. The 'hog's back' showed that early farmers were sincere in their search to find a threshing method which would limit the damage done to the grain. The 'back' consisted of a series of spikes set in a board through which the sheaf was pulled. But the introduction of the flail saw a solution to the problem which was to last for centuries, and indeed it is known that use was being made of the flail in remoter parts of Scotland in the early years of this century. A flail was made of a staff of wood up to five feet in length – ash or larch were commonly used – and a shorter 'souple' or threshing arm, the two being joined together by a short length of hide or rope. The threshing was accomplished by placing one line of sheaves side by side on the barn floor and laying a further line on top in the opposite direction in such a way that the heads overlapped. Swinging the flail over his shoulder, the worker would beat his way down the line. The sheaves would then be turned and a further flailing given. The *Scottish Gallovidian Encyclopaedia* of 1824 gives an unusual insight into a barn dance called 'Brannan's Jig':

> *This is a dance which those persons have who thresh with the flail. The 'souple' on the end of the hand-staff being whirled round on the barn floor by the barnman; every wheel he gives it, he leaps over it, and so produces a very singular dance, worth walking a mile to see, yet few of the barnmen who do this dance in style, are willing to perform before spectators. The girl who*

cleans the corn is the only one for common who is
gratified with the sight.

The first attempts at mechanical harvesting were based on
a number of flails attached to a rotating axle, but gradually
more effective practices evolved. Then in 1787, Andrew
Meikle, an ingenious millwright from East Lothian, and
son of James Meikle who designed the first winnower,
devised a machine which revolutionised the operation, its
principles even today making a contribution to mechanical
harvesting. Meikle used a combination of rollers, a
revolving drum and beaters to detach the seeds and husks,
and wirework and winnowing separations on the basis
of size and density. By this time there were no religious
prejudices against the creation of a current of air in a
machine for the blowing aside of light particles –
remember what Sir Walter Scott wrote about fanning
attempts in *Old Mortality*:

> *Your leddyship and the steward hae been pleased to*
> *propose that my son Cuddie suld work in the barn wi'*
> *a new-fangled machine for dighting the corn frae the*
> *chaff, thus impiously thwarting the will of Divine*
> *Providence, by raising wind for your leddyship's ain*
> *particular use by human art, instead of soliciting it by*
> *prayer, or waiting patiently for whatever dispensation*
> *of wind Providence was pleased to send upon the*
> *sheeling-hill.*

Meikle's mill was quickly taken up all over Scotland,
England and Europe and became a common item of barn
equipment. But the farm mill often did not have the
capacity to thresh out more than a few days' requirements
and in due course one of the great sights of the countryside
was to arrive on the scene – the travelling mill, pulled, first
of all by a team of horses and later by an enormous steam
traction engine. A travelling mill meant the services of a
large gang was required; traditionally neighbours came to
help and the farmer's wife had a large-scale catering job on

her hands. Perhaps most of the enjoyment went to the dogs, careering after the vermin sneaking out from the stacks being fed into the mill. Certainly today's Health and Safety Executive would have had a field-day condemning the unguarded drive belts which linked engine and mill. Nor would the remedy for a slipping belt – an application of horse treacle – have found much favour.

Today, of course, the majestic combine-harvester, probably operated by a contractor, cuts and threshes in one operation. Gone are the stooks and stackyards, where children played. The grain will be dried and stored in silos until required for processing. The straw will be baled for easy storing. But the golden crops of oats are unchanging; they still bend and wave in the wind, touching the senses, linking today with what has gone before.

Corn Rigs, Lea Rigs and End Rigs

> *Corn rigs, an' barley rigs,*
> *An' corn rigs are bonie:*
> *I'll ne'er forget that happy night,*
> *Amang the rigs wi' Annie.*
> 'Corn Rigs are Bonie', Robert Burns, 1759-1796

Dry-stane dykes are common enough sights in Scotland. It was not always so. In the Middle Ages movement across the land was not hindered by dykes, fences or hedges. Most people lived in villages and the run-rig system of farming was in operation. This meant that ground capable of supporting crops was divided into strips or ridges with ownership or tenancy of the strips being divided amongst different people, so that it was unusual for one man to have possession of adjoining strips. The strips came into being because of the nature of the cultivation. The absence of field drains encouraged cultivation which raised the level of the crop-bearing ground, leaving ground at a lower level between the ridges to act as an open drain. Even today it is common to see land, especially on hill-sides,

13

showing regular, if gentle corrugations across fields, indicating its past cropping in ridges, or rigs as they came to be called. Fergusson seemed to find profit in the run-rig system:

> *That fruits and herbage may our farm adorn,*
> *And furrowed ridges teem with loaded corn.*
> 'Pastoral', Robert Fergusson, 1750-1774

To us, it seems the system barely warranted the term subsistence.

The breadth of a rig was normally between five and ten metres; its length depended on the make-up of the soil and the slope of the ground. It is known that the rigs frequently were rotated between different farmers to give more equitable income opportunities. The best land was kept for the growing of crops while the poorer ground was occupied by stock. Arable and grazing ground were thus distinct.

The change from the run-rig system to self-contained farming units was a natural progression encouraged by a number of different circumstances and took many years to evolve. More mouths to feed as the population increased demanded that more crops be grown, and this was done at the expense of the grazing ground. The opportunity to develop a cattle trade with England required more winter feeding for the stock, and the number of barns and byres had to be increased. These were built near to the best crop carrying ground so that the manure did not have to be moved further than necessary. Thus came the development of the 'in-bye' (or 'muckit land') and the out-fields which might be cropped or grazed. But as Henry Grey Graham points out in the *Social Life of Scotland in the Eighteenth Century* (1899), husbandry was still at a pitiful level:

> *The land attached to each farm was divided into 'infield'*
> *and 'outfield'; that nearest the house being the croft or*
> *'infield' to which all the care was devoted . . . Six times*
> *larger than the 'infield' was the 'outfield', – wretched,*
> *ill-kept, untended ground, each portion of which was put*
> *perpetually into oats, or, more usually, for three years in*

succession; and thereafter it lay for another three or four years, or even six years fallow, acquiring a rich 'natural grass' of weeds, moss, thistles, on which the horses, sheep and black cattle fed. Ground was cultivated till it produced only two seeds for every one sown; the third year being called the 'wersh crop', as it was miserable alike in quantity and in quality. Still, however, in spite of all disastrous experience of centuries people clung to their ancient system, and their faith was embalmed in those popular wise saws which condense so much popular stupidity:

'If land be three years out and three years in,
T'will keep in good heart till the deil grow blin'.

The introduction of field drains eliminated the need to have land lying uncultivated between ridges, and this land was gradually brought under the plough. Wheat began to be grown, and, as it required winter sowing as opposed to the then spring sowing of oats and barley, the cultivated ground had to be protected by dykes or hedges from livestock which normally would have been feeding on the in-bye ground at that time of the year. In time, the fertility of the out-bye land was raised until as much of the farm as possible came into a rotation of crops including grass or lea. Where possible, oats came after lea in a rotation, as no crop does better on ploughed up turf.

When ploughing a field, of course, the furrow could not be run to the edge of the field, as space had to be left for the horses to turn before ploughing again in the reverse direction. It was this space at the end of the field that was known as the end-rig, the last bit of ground to be ploughed.

2
Milling

When I was a miller in Fife,
Losh! I thought that the sound o' the happer
Said, Tak hame a wee flow to your wife,
To help to be brose to your supper.
Then my conscience was narrow and pure;
But, someway, by random it rackit;
Fir I lifted twa nievfu or mair,–
While the happer said, Tak' it, man, tak it.

'Tak' it, Man, Tak' it', David Webster, 1787-1837

Some of the earliest references to milling are contained in the Bible where we discover that people ground manna in mills, or beat it in a mortar. In Judges 16:21, we learn that after Samson had been taken by the Philistines, 'he did grind in the prison house'. St Matthew comments on the two women grinding at the mill, 'the one taken and the other left.' For a more detailed study of early milling with religious connections, an examination of *Vita Sancti Columbae*, the biography of Columba written by his fellow monk, Adamnan, proves profitable. Here we glean the quite fascinating information that not only did the monks use hand-grinding implements, but they also built a kiln for drying their corn and experimented with a water-driven mill – all this around the year 700 AD.

Earliest methods of milling were no doubt the 'knocking stone' where the grain was beaten in some kind of stone crucible with a pounding instrument, and the rolling of a round or cylindrical shape over a flat or slightly concave stone on which grain had been spread. Such stones, dated around 1500 BC have been found in Strathclyde. But the big leap forward in milling technology came with the introduction of querns, and their importance was recognised by the Israelites who were forbidden to seize them for debt, the command being: 'No man shall take the upper or the lower millstone to pledge: for he taketh the man's life to pledge.'

Querns were certainly being used in Scotland when the Romans arrived. Indeed, querns provided such a beautiful and elegant solution to the problem of milling that in many parts of the country there were no further improvements for centuries. They were, in fact, still in use in the north of Scotland, Orkney and Shetland at the beginning of the present century, although Boswell on his Highland journey with Dr Johnson seemed to think they were already outdated:

> Saturday 25th September 1773
> We stopped at a little hut, where we saw an old woman
> grinding with the quern, the ancient Highland
> instrument, which it is said was used by the Romans,
> but which, being very slow in its operation, is almost
> entirely gone into disuse.

It is by no means uncommon today to find a quern stone lying in a farm steading. A quern consisted of two circular flat stones, the upper one pierced in the centre with a hole or funnel and revolving on a pin inserted in the lower. The upper stone was sometimes ornamented. In using the quern, the oats were fed into the central opening while the upper stone was revolved by means of a stick inserted into it near the edge. Grooves were cut on the underside of the top stones and these encouraged the ground oats to move out, and over the edge of the quern. Initially the ground meal was collected from a cloth on the ground on which the quern was sited. In *Scottish Life and Character,* William Sanderson makes a seldom encountered reference to a 'quern-lilt':

> The quern grinding was preceded by the heating of the
> corn in an iron pot, or by some similar contrivance, and
> as soon as the grain was crisp enough the two stones
> were brought into use. Two women, who sat facing each
> other on the ground, generally acted as millers. Into the
> side of the upper stone which has a hole in the centre, a
> wooden handle was fixed, and the stone was turned by
> means of this handle being pushed from one to the other,
> the corn being poured from time to time into the hole
> at the top. The monotonous action was generally
> accompanied by a low crooning song or quern-lilt,
> which suggests the customs of Eastern women, who
> 'warbled as they ground the parched corn'.

'Scottish Life and Character', William Sanderson, 1904

In later years, the quern was placed on a stand, allowing the meal to be collected in a hopper arrangement. Made of skin, a hopper is a storage receptacle, often funnel-shaped. As time progressed, larger stones were brought into use, with animals providing the necessary power, and by the end of the eleventh century, water mills were introduced.

Man has long had an interest in using water as a source of power. The water wheel was known in ancient Egypt where it was used to raise water for irrigation purposes. Scotland, with its multitude of swift-flowing rivers and streams, offered easy conditions for simple damming where a head of water could be built up. How many water mills were built we shall never know but the number must have been prodigious. Regrettably, only a few water mills have been maintained in a working condition, the present fashion being to convert them into luxury homes or hotels. But where they are still to be seen in operation, such as Rogers' Mill at Aberfeldy, the public heads for them with the enthusiasm of little boys rushing to see traction engines. Yet, having said that, one notable personage had little enthusiasm for water mills. Sir Walter Scott, writing in his diary on 10 February 1827, records:

> *I do not know why, but from my childhood I have seen something fearful, or melancholy at least, about a mill. Whether I had been frightened at the machinery when very young, of which I think I have some shadowy remembrance – whether I had heard the stories of the Miller of Thirlstane, and similar molendinar tragedies, I cannot tell; but not even recollections of the Lass of Patie's Mill, or the Miller of Mansfield, or 'he who dwelt on the River Dee' have ever got over my inclination to connect gloom with a mill, especially when the sun is setting.*

It is surprising that, even in the windier parts of Scotland, windmills do not appear to have been all that common, although a few were known to be operating in Aberdeenshire and in Orkney in the sixteenth and seventeenth centuries. Returning Crusaders are generally given the credit for introducing windmills into Europe, but we have to wait until 1750 before we can claim Scottish ingenuity at the fore when Andrew Meikle, whose name we continually encounter in the study of farming and milling, devised an improved method of moving the vanes to catch the wind. In some parts of the country, particularly around Inverness, Aberdeen and on the Forth at Burntisland and Musselburgh, attempts were made by forward-thinking pioneers to drive mills by tidal power, but no great success was obtained.

It must be remembered that first attempts at milling resulted in the outer coat of the oat, known as the husk or shell, being mixed with the groat or inner kernel which alone gives oatmeal. There was, then, a need to separate this mixture of husks and groats so that the latter could be ground into meal. One primitive method adopted was to throw the mixture into the air at a windy place from a basket known as a 'wecht' allowing the torn shells to blow away while the heavier groats fell to the ground where they were collected on sheets spread out for the purpose. This method of separating the mealie groats from the shells gave rise to the name 'Shielhill', still a fairly common place-name, especially for a farm, in Scotland. The 'shiel', of course, is the shell from the oats, and the Shielhill is the windy hill where the winnowing took place.

A later improvement on this inevitably wasteful method of separation was to site the barn in such a way as to make use of the prevailing wind. Doors on opposite sides of the barn would be opened to provide a wind channel and, as the grain was tossed up, the chaff and other light material would be carried away.

In 1710, Andrew Fletcher of Saltoun, having become sickened of politics, was devoting his energies to agricul-tural improvement. He had seen milling operations on the Continent, and sent his wheelwright, James Meikle over to Holland to gain ideas for improvement at home. On top of his shilling-a-day wages and a similar sum for entertainment, the noble Saltoun promised Meikle's wife a payment of five pounds sterling should Meikle lose his life in the enterprise and journey. Meikle returned from Holland with the successful design of a 'fanner' to separate groats and shells. Unfortunately, one cannot please all of the people all of the time. The religiously inclined accused Meikle of contravening scripture by 'making the Devil's wind' and the adoption of the fanner was a slow process.

As mills became more sophisticated, additional stones were added so that one set of stones would first remove the shell and the second set would grind the groats into meal of the desired cut.

It is difficult to mill soft or moist grain and frequently drying is required. The earliest and most primitive method of drying was known as 'graddaning' which merely involved setting fire to the ears of the oats and burning them off the stalks. The burned ears would then be hand rubbed or trodden before winnowing and the dried oats then milled in the quern. That ace reporter Boswell lets us know that the primitive method long existed in parts of Scotland:

9th September 1773
At breakfast this morning, among a profusion of other
things, there were oatcakes, made of what is called
graddaned meal, that is, meal made of grain separated
from the husks, and toasted by fire, instead of being
threshed and kiln dried. This seemed to be bad
management, as so much fodder is consumed by it.
Mr. McQueen however defended it by saying that it is
doing the thing much quicker, as one operation effects
what is otherwise done by two. His chief reason however
was, that the servants in Skye are, according to him, a
faithless pack and steal what they can; so much is saved
by the corn passing but once through their hands as at
each time they pilfer some.

Other simple methods of drying involved the use of pots or
heated stones. Nevertheless, kilns made an early entry onto
the scene. The Romans were acquainted with them and they
were also the subject of legislation in the Middle Ages. Early
kilns were simple stone structures – smaller in the north
than in the Lowlands – and consisted of a fire chamber from
which the heat went up a flue to a slatted drying floor on
which the oats were spread, probably on top of straw. By the
early 1800s, wire-cloth on iron bars was becoming a more
common floor arrangement. Today's sophisticated kilns may
be either horizontally or vertically positioned and they dry
the oats moving through heated areas, the oats being
continuously turned to ensure even drying. Much emphasis
is placed by millers on the drying process as it bears so
strongly on the flavour of the final product.

As the size and number of stones used in milling
increased, so did their 'dressing' become more of a craft. It
was the job of the stone dresser to cut grooves of the
correct size and angle in the stones to ensure that the
meal did not choke the mill when it was being ground, and
to help it find its way to the outside edge of the stones for
collection. At first, stones for milling were obtained from
nearby quarries; later, the sandstone from the Derbyshire
Peak District found favour for the top, revolving stone.

Eventually, though, every commercial mill used 'buhr', a hard, flinty stone imported from France. These 'buhr' stones were long-lasting – their surfaces wore down much more slowly than other stones. It is said that because of their importance, a trade embargo with France was lifted for three months during the Napoleonic era so that they could be imported.

For many years in Scotland, the milling of oats was the cause of much friction between farmer and landlord. When building a mill, the laird took action to make sure it would be profitable. The measure taken was called 'thirlage' and involved the inclusion in the lease of a clause which stated the tenant had to have his crops ground at the laird's mill. And to, as they say, 'mak siccar' (make sure) the tenant might also have to dispose of his quern.

Leglislation to force tenants to use the mills of their 'superiors' can be traced back to a decree issued by Alexander III:

> *Nae man, sall presume to grind quekit, mash-lock, or*
> *rye, hand-mylne, except he be compelled by storme, or*
> *bein lack of mills, quihilk soulde grinde the samen; and*
> *in this case, gif a man grindes at hand-Mylnes, he sall*
> *gif the threllin measure as milture; gif any man*
> *contraveins this, our proclamation, he sall tyne his*
> *mill perpetuallie.*

Sanderson's Scottish Life and Character,1919

If this was not harsh enough, additional clauses in the 'thirlage' agreement sometimes obliged the tenant to help in the maintenance of the mill, as well as its dam and lade. This obviously was not, and could not become, a long-term happy relationship. It was a custom, also, for payment to be made to the miller in the form of a proportion of the meal; this was known as 'multure'. In 1796, the miller at the water mill working today at Aberfeldy, not only received multures from each tenant but at Christmas had to be provided with a mutton ham. Not surprisingly, there arose many arguments over the weight of oats sent to the mill, the apparent loss of weight during milling, the quantity of meal produced and so on. Even where the tenant did not send his oats to his own laird's mill, he was obliged to make a standing payment, and legal action might be taken against any tenant seeking to avoid payment. These payments, in some cases, had to be paid in perpetuity and, with the demise of the country mill, have led to more than a few squabbles.

The miller then was understandably not the most popular person in a community. But, if we are to believe our poetry and prose, his assured income became a point of envy as the years passed and many a girl saw herself in her contemplative moments, enjoying the comfortable life of a miller's wife. Sir John Clerk in the first part of the eighteenth century said it rather nicely:

> *Merry may the maid be*
> *That marries a miller;*
> *For, foul day and fair day,*
> *He's aye bringing till her,*
> *Has aye a penny in his purse*
> *For dinner and for supper;*
> *And, gin she please, a good fat cheese*
> *And lumps of yellow butter.*
>
> *In winter when the wind and rain*
> *Blaws o'er the house and byre,*
> *He sits beside a clean heart-stane*
> *Before a rousin' fire:*
> *With nut brown ale he tells his tale,*
> *Which rows him o'er fu' nappy:*
> *Who'd be a king – a petty thing,*
> *When a miller lives so happy."*

'The Miller', Sir John Clerk, 1680-1755

The miller and his love-life has entered our folklore to an unusual degree. Allan Ramsay and Burns have both had something to say about him, while Scott Skinner based compositions around the 'Miller O' Hirn' and the 'Miller O'Logie'. 'The Auld Meal Mill' has warmed many a bothy night although the modern words possess not the couthiness of Mackie's original:

> *An yestreen, when in the shadow o' its ivy covered wa's,*
> *I vow'd I'd leave my mither, ere the fleece o' winter fa's,*
> *An' she'll no withhaud her blessin', when I gang ayont*
>   *the hill,*
> *There tae wed an' bide wi' Jamie, at the auld meal mill.*

Life was not all roses however around the meal mill. To a miller's wife goes the credit of killing one of the last wolves in Scotland. The lady was working in the kitchen when the animal entered, making for the cradle where her baby was sleeping. Grabbing a wooden utensil, the miller's wife repeatedly struck the wolf on the head. Today, the place bears the name 'Mullinavaddie' – the mill of the wolf.

Today's oatmeal mill is a highly complex affair which still demands the craftsman's touch if a high-class product is to be obtained. On arrival from the harvest field, the grain is first weighed, then quality-control checked for such things as colour, size and weight of kernel. It is dried, if necessary and subjected to an initial cleaning process to remove straw and other items which may have been picked up during harvesting. Then it is stored in silos capable of holding thousands of tons of oats so that the production of meal may continue through the year.

From the silos the grain undergoes further cleaning to separate the light and small oats and husks, and this is done by passing the oats over and through a series of sieves and aspirators. More difficult to separate out are weed seeds similar in size and density to the grain which, if milled with the grain, would produce unwelcome coloured particles in the meal. Special equipment for working on the surface adhesiveness of the weed seeds may be used for this operation, although some exciting work has been done in recent years, separating oats from other seeds by means of electronically operated colour separators.

The kilning of oats is normally the next step, although there are millers who prefer to remove the husks before kilning. This, it can be argued, is the most important operation of all, as it is the kilning that brings out the flavour and aroma which make oatmeal products unique. Further re-grading will follow before the naked kernel or groat passes to the cutters or rollers or stones to produce the texture of meal required. This may be the chunky pinhead, coarse, medium or fine oatmeal.

In 1877 the American Quaker Oat Company launched flaked oats on to the market and the ease of their preparation has made them a favourite breakfast food world-wide. When flaking, standardisation of size is important; it is now common practice to use a specialist machine to cut the groat into three or four parts before the steaming process and before the oats are fed through large heavy rollers; cooling and packing follows. There is also a movement today towards the flaking of the whole groat for porridge-making and biscuit-making purposes, a consumer-led demand perhaps for more 'bite' in the product.

Travelling mill hauled by steam traction engine.

Three-horse teams at work in the harvest field.

Corn peerie (or dolly) decorating the crown of a stack.

Winnowing oats in Shetland c.1900.

Leading oats from field to stackyard.

Bothy lads in Angus.

Bakehouse. Note the hot iron table used for baking the oatcakes.

Broadcasting oats.

Scything.

Cutting oats with a binder.

Bothy interior.

Utensils used for making porridge and oatcakes.

A line of corn stacks.

Grinding
corn in
a quern.

Gathering feed for horses during the Boer War.

Stooks of oats.

3
Weights and Measures

Nor dribbles o' drink rins through the draff,
Nor pickles o' meal rins through the Mill-e'e'.
'Werna My Heart Licht', Lady Grisell Baillie, 1665-1746

A Guid New-Year I wish thee, Maggie!
Hae, there's a ripp to thy auld baggie.
'The Auld Farmer's New-Year Morning Salutation
to His Auld Mare, Maggie', Robert Burns, 1786

The Scots tongue is rich in terms which, though they may
be unknown to the listener, are so descriptive that they
immediately call their meaning to mind. A 'pickle of meal'
is a case in point; it just has to be a small quantity flowing
through the fingers. Similarly, the 'ripp' of corn given to
the old horse in Burns' lines conjures up the picture of
a handful of oats being pulled through splayed fingers
from a sheaf lying in the barn. Such terms as 'pickle' and
'ripp' are a reminder of the old vocabulary of weights
and measures that existed long before a metric or even an
Imperial system was introduced. Many of the old Scots
weight and measure terms were the same as those used in
England but often the actual weight or measure differed.
For example, a Scots peck was about eight pounds (8 lbs),
while the English peck was a pound more than that.
Indeed, it seems likely that even within Scotland the
weight or measure accorded to a particular term might
vary from place to place.

As well as responding to the market forces of supply and demand, the established way of putting a monetary value on a sample of oats was first by physical examination. In the old corn markets, it was a common sight to see millers and grain merchants examining a sample of oats brought in by a farmer for appearance, colour, smell and lack of mould and admixtures. Then would come the calculating of the sample's bushel weight on a small portable bushel measure as this gave an indication as to the amount of oatmeal that might be extracted from the oats on offer (the higher the bushel weight, the greater the extraction). A bushel is a measure of volume and the original standard weight given to a bushel of oats was forty pounds (40 lbs), later to be increased to forty-two pounds. The weight of a bushel of oats depended, and still does of course, largely on the plumpness of the grain, although it is affected by how well light oats, empty husks and so on have been removed from the sample. The estimation of the oats' moisture content (for no-one likes to pay for water) was a question of feel in the hand.

Such practice is considered too subjective in today's world of high technology. Most crops are grown on a contract basis between farmer and supplier to an agreed price arrangement and with set standards of quality. Moisture content is calculated scientifically. Oatmeal millers today demand a full and elongated groat and it is the 'husk to groat' ratio that is important. While bushel weight is not without value, it is taken after screening a sample to remove light oats and trash, or extraction tests may be carried out. This is a far remove from Dean Ramsay's story of the Scots farmer holidaying in England who approached a young girl reaping with a sickle in a field of oats:

'Lassie, are yer aits muckle bookit th' year?'
'Sir!' was the response.
'I' was speiring gif yer aits are muckle bookit th' year.'
'I really don't know what you are saying sir.'
'– Gude – safe – us,– do ye no understaan gude plain

28

English! – are – yer – aits – muckle bookit?'
'Reminiscences of Scottish Life and Character',
Sir A Geikie, 1904

Oats, however, were not traded in such small quantities as bushels but in a measure known as a 'quarter' which was eight bushels. When the Corn Sales Act was passed in 1921, whereby all oats had to be sold by weight, the quarter became standardised at three hundredweights. Three hundredweights can hardly be lifted by one person and the practice evolved of weighing oats into sacks of half that weight, that is a hundredweight-and-a-half, known to add to the confusion, as half-a-quarter. The position was even worse with wheat and barley. Due to their higher bushel weight, half-a-quarter of barley weighed two hundredweights, and a half quarter of wheat, two-and-a-quarter-hundredweights. Stacking bags of those weights, frequently three high, or eight high if the bags were laid flat on top of each other was killing work and many mill workers aged before their time. When a mill changed over to bulk handling there were cheers all round.

Having taken receipt of his oats in quarters, the miller would then sell his meal by a measurement known as a 'boll', a term still in use today. This unit was standardised at ten stones, that is, 140 pounds. A typical allowance of meal given to a married farm servant was half a boll a month, while a single man living in the bothy would receive a 'firlot', half the married man's allowance.

A measure frequently used when dishing out oats for the work horses was the 'lippie' which weighed a pound-and-three-quarters. In the days when a farm servant was allowed garden ground for growing his kail he would be given what was known as a 'lippie-sowing' – an area of ground equivalent to what would be covered by broadcasting a lippie of seed.

4
Porridge

The healsome Parritch, chief o' Scotia's food
'The Cotter's Saturday Night', Robert Burns, 1786

On sicken food has mony a doughty deed
by Caledonia's ancestors been done.
'The Farmer's Ingle', Robert Fergusson, 1771

In many Scottish households the changing of the clock in
October heralds the re-introduction of porridge on the
breakfast table. It is a sensible tradition, for few, if any,
breakfast dishes give greater fortification against the cold.

The spelling of the word seems to have been settled
around the end of the eighteenth century. Prior to that time
a variety of spellings were in use: 'parrage' and 'parritge'
were common and literature up to the end of the sixteenth
century makes reference to 'porrage' and inevitably 'porage',
the descriptive term used by one major manufacturer (A &
R Scott) today. According to many dictionaries, porridge is
a mixture of oatmeal and water which undergoes a boiling
and simmering treatment. Salt is a necessary additive and
the true Scot deplores its replacement, as is frequently done
south of the Border, by sugar.

For hundreds of years porridge was the staple food of
the poorer people in Scotland. Personalised as 'they', in
many households, the porridge pot was never moved from
the fireside and the eating of porridge while standing up

was always an acceptable custom. At the table two bowls would be used, one filled with porridge and the other with milk. Rather than milk being poured over the porridge, it was customary for each spoonful to be dipped into the milk bowl before eating. Milk, however, was not necessarily the only accompaniment to porridge. Honey, syrup and treacle were popular and there are records indicating that ale and porter were not without their devotees. Old porridge bowls were normally made of wood and the spoon was made from horn which did not transmit heat to the mouth so readily. The stirring of porridge was, and of course still is, done using a long, tapered stick, often with a carved head and known, according to locality, as a 'spurtle' or 'thrievel'. The stirring of porridge, of course, is always done in a clockwise direction to ensure good luck.

William Miller, the nineteenth-century poet who has delighted the generations with 'Wee Willie Winkie', knew that porridge was the focal point of the morning:

> *Are ye no gaun to wauken the-day, ye rogue?*
> *Your parritch is ready, and cool in the cog;*
> *Auld baudrons sae gaucy, and Tam o' that ilk,*
> *Would fain hae a drap o' the wee laddie's milk.*
> *So, up to your parritch, and on wi' your claes! –*
> *There's a fire that might warm ye cauld Norlan' braes;*
> *For a coggie weel fill'd and a clean fire-en*
> *Should mak' ye jump up and gae skelping ben!*
>
> 'The Sleepy, Sleepy, Laddie', William Miller, 1810-1872

In the days when many, many more workers lodged on the farm than ever happens today, it was customary for a farm servant to use two 'kists' or chests. Blankets were kept in one and meal in the other. In order to retain its condition, the meal had to be tightly packed, an operation which involved rolling up the trouser legs and trampling inside the kist with bare feet. In the bothies of the old 'farm touns' where the single men and sometimes, to the chagrin of the Auld Kirk, the single women also were accommodated, porridge was known to be given a variation that would startle the most fervent oatmeal fanatic of today. Before taking to the fields, the farm servant would ladle some porridge into a drawer of a chest where it would cool off. At night it would be sliced into chunks and, rejoicing under its new name of 'calders', would supplement an egg or fish dish.

How well a farm servant ate depended much on the kindliness of the farmer. But many would have thought they were born into the wrong era if they ever read Scott's *Old Mortality*:

> *On the day after Cuddie's arrival, Robin placed on the table an immense charger of broth, thickened with oatmeal and colewort, in which ocean of liquid was indistinctly discovered two or three short ribs of lean mutton sailing to and fro. Two huge baskets, one of bread made of barley and pease, and one of oatcakes flanked this standing dish.*

A further confirmation, this time from the Highlands, that some were fortunate enough to start the day in style comes from Sir Archibald Geikie :

> *There are few meals in the world more enjoyable than a true Highland breakfast. The porridge and cream at the beginning provide a sensible substratum on which the later viands can be built up. Even if you confine your efforts to only one or two of these viands, the variety of the whole table, redolent of the hillside and the moor, and so unlike the typical morning repast of ordinary southerners, inserts a sense of plenty and freedom.*
>
> 'Reminiscences of Scottish Life and Character', Sir A Geikie, 1904

In the seventeenth century though, things were not so good for the ordinary folk – Douglas describes the diet of farmers and servants in his *Description of the East Coast of Scotland*:

> *Breakfast – oatmeal porridge with milk or ale, or broth made of cabbage left overnight, and oat bannock.*
> *Dinner – Sowans, with milk and oatcake or kail.*
> *Supper at seven during winter, or nine in summer – kail [cabbage], with oatcakes.*

But, to return to more normal circumstances. In the pre-oatflake era it took time, of course, to make porridge, an overnight steeping of the meal being common. And when time was short, the answer was to make brose. The pouring of boiling water over oatmeal, the addition of salt, and often pepper, was all that was required to prepare this meal, which was then eaten as gruel with milk over it. Because the oatmeal was not cooked it was not swollen when eaten; so a man could be taking to the fields with a huge weight of meal in his stomach. No wonder breakfast was consumed standing up; it was the easiest way for the meal to go down. What is remarkable, is that so many 'bothy ballads' and legends testify to the fact that the taste of this simply made dish depended on who had made it. Some farms were sought for the quality of their brose – some had to be avoided. As always there was a rhymer:

> Gie me ma brose – ma aitmeal brose,
> Weel buttered an' weel steered.
> Wi' kail or cabbage bree intil't –
> Or ream, gin't can be spared!
>
> Gie me ma brose, sin Mother Eve
> Pree'd that forbidden apple,
> Na finer, sweeter, healthier fare
> Has crossed owre mortal thrapple.

Traditional

Another famous variation of porridge was known as 'sowans' – a dish which Dr Johnson consumed heartily at Tobermory on his Highland journey.

To make sowans, 'sids' (the inner husks of the oats with kernels sticking to them) would be steeped in twice their bulk of water for a week or so until the mixture became sour. The liquid would be drained off and fresh water and salt added to the sediment which was then boiled until it became rich and creamy. Sometimes the sediment itself would be worked into a dough and rolled in oatmeal. This was a regular school 'piece' for children and, because sowans kept well, was a favourite food when going on a long journey. In the days of farm touns, sowans were often mixed with milk, or when milk was scarce in the winter-time, with ale, and carried to the field in the inevitable lemonade bottle. Sanderson in his, *Scottish Life and Character* quotes an Englishman's comments on sowans to his friends after returning south: 'The lady of the house boiled some dirty water in a pan, and by the blessing of God it came out a fine pudding.'

Understandably, the eating of all this oatmeal food was claimed to produce the skin disease 'Scotch fiddle', so named because of the continual scratching it promoted:

> *Our sturdy Scottish Ancestors*
> *Were hairy round the knees;*
> *With voices gruff they took their snuff*
> *And never stopped to sneeze;*
> *They supped their porridge to a man,*
> *With salt in it, and knots,*
> *And shook their beards in horror*
> *If their sons came out in spots.*
>
> Traditional

The accepted cure for 'Scotch Fiddle' was a diet of pease-meal brose.

In old Scots books where the humour of the day was to the fore, pawky comments about food were common. Robert Ford in *Thistledown* produces this example:

> *'Jock,' cried a farmer's wife to her cowherd, 'come awa in to your parritch, or the flees'll be droonin' themsel's in your milk bowl.'*
>
> *'Nae fear o' that,' was Jock's reply. 'They'll wade through.'*
>
> *'Ye scoondrel', cried his mistress, 'd'ye mean to say that ye dinna get eneuch milk?'*
>
> *'Ou, ay,' said Jock, 'I get plenty o' milk for a the Parritch'.*
>
> 'Thistledown', Robert Ford, 1913

Porridge, today, is regarded as a first breakfast dish (before the bacon and eggs), and has been considerably sophisticated as a morning cereal. Most porridge makers today use flaked oats which involve a minimum of effort and cooking time. Some diehards, though, will continue to buy medium oatmeal and steep it overnight, arguing it has a better flavour. What continues to surprise is the export trade for oats to warmer climates. It seems the ubiquitous Scot finds nothing incongruous in eating hot porridge in the tropics.

5
Oatcakes

The best o' bannocks tae yer tea
Gangs doon yer craig like leaves in spate.
  'The Guidwife Speaks', Violet Jacob, 1863-1946

The current enthusiasm for health foods is happily
increasing the popularity of oatcakes. High in nutritional
value, their substantial fibre content provides a balancing
roughage to some of our high-cholesterol foods. But
whether the accompanying food is 'party fayre' or cheese
or honey, oatcakes are the perfect partner. They have the
ability to go with any food, even ice-cream (an introduction which must be credited to the Americans),
although Burns' liking for eating them with warm ale is
more understandable. Oatcakes, today, are exported to all
parts of the world, with Canada, no doubt because of its
large Scottish immigrant population, possibly being the
largest market. But food-conscious France takes its quota,
the Bretons showing a particular partiality for the product.
Indeed a BBC interviewer talking recently to a fairly
well known French chef in a London hotel asked him
what British food he thought should be more widely
consumed in France. His answer came back with speed
and conviction – 'Scots oatcakes'.

Soldiering has always been a popular Scottish vocation,
and in the Middle Ages Scottish soldiers were renowned
for their ability to travel quickly and fight lustily on an

apparently meagre diet. Froissart, the great European traveller and historian of the fourteenth century (and perhaps the first ever war correspondent having, it is suspected, ridden with Border rievers), sets out in his writings:

> *Under the flap of his saddle, each man carries a broad plate of metal; behind the saddle a little bag of oatmeal. They place this plate over the fire, mix with water their oatmeal, and when the plate is heated, they put a little of the paste upon it, and make a thin cake, like a cracknel or biscuit, which they eat to warm their stomachs.*

> 'Froissart's Chronicles', trans. Col Johnson, 1803

Thus is set out the first recipe for oatcakes. The relationship between the Scots fighting man and his oatcakes is obviously one that continued over the centuries, for we read that a patriotic Highland lady, upon learning of the defeat of Bonnie Prince Charlie's army by the Duke of Cumberland at Culloden, set up a roadside stall providing fresh oatmeal bannocks for men making their escape from the battlefield. It seems the Scot may be caricatured for his meanness or love of whisky or haggis, but when it comes to his meal, more than a note of seriousness is evident.

Well into the present century it was a farmhouse custom for a large mix of oatmeal dough to be prepared weekly and stretched out over a rope to dry, allowing the cook, in due course, to tear off appropriate strips to put on the girdle.

The part of the country one is in determines whether the term 'bannock' is synonymous with 'oatcake'. In western parts the words are interchangeable, whilst in the east and north-east in particular the bannock may contain a proportion of wheat flour, and is an item for the sweeter-toothed. Indeed, in those areas, the description of being a cross between an oatcake and a digestive biscuit is not a bad one. While the name 'farl' lingers on, the original product, unfortunately, does not. A farl was a large oatcake baked slowly only on the one side to bring out the full flavour of the oatmeal. As it cooled, the edges curled up, not a suitable shape for present-day packaging.

But, of course, all oatcakes do not taste the same, and the connoisseur can point to their variations, subtle and otherwise, in the same way as the whisky drinker contrasts a malt from Islay with one from Speyside. It has been said said 'There's no such thing as bad whisky, it's just that some are better than others' and such a view can equally be applied to oatcakes; the ingredients are far too honest for them to do a person other than good.

The amount of kiln drying or toasting given somewhere in the total process will bear upon the nuttiness of the flavour possessed by the oatcake. They may be baked to varying degrees of hardness and many bakers have their own 'secret' ingredient which they add to give their product something distinctive; an extra measure of salt, or a pinch of sugar or shortening, extra bran, some malt; why should we not welcome their efforts to appease our palates? Important, too, is the degree of coarseness of the oatmeal used. I well remember my first visit to Orkney when I could not decide which of the two largest selling oatcakes I preferred, although they were as different as chalk and cheese. One was large, bold and rough; the other refined and gentle. This question of texture is an important one today. Most oatcakes are sold through supermarkets and these organisations keep a firm check on the turnover of lines and allocate space accordingly. The accurate feedback they can give on customer preference and changing tastes is of immense value to the oatcake manufacturer. Not that that necessarily makes life easier for the manufacturer, regional pockets of difference in a national market will always exist.

As a generalisation, the largest demand is for a fairly rough oatcake with a good bite to it, when coarse oatmeal, or perhaps a mixture of pinhead and medium, will be favourite constituents, with the odd small bakery producing a particularly rough oatcake from a meal specially milled for the purpose. In the more northern parts of Scotland, the demand is for a floury type of oatcake made from finely ground oats which more readily form a dough. Thanks, at least in part, to the healthy eating fashion, now in vogue, the English market continues to grow, and our southern brethren are opting in the main for finer oatcakes. Many supermarkets, of course, like to offer oatcakes under their own label, using the manufacturing expertise of major oatcake manufacturers. While the manufacturer may have mixed views on this trend, depending whether or not he is getting the business, there are customer benefits to be obtained, as long as a healthy balance between supermarket brand and manufacturers' brands is maintained. The advantage is the supermarket can provide its own recipe to meet its particular needs, be it for more sweeter-toothed customers in an area, or, for oatcakes of a different size and shape.

The traditional shape for an oatcake is akin to a triangle, being the result of quartering a large circular cake on a girdle so that it could be lifted off with a spathe. A large triangle is not a favourite consumer's shape as it breaks if a knife is applied to it as it lies on a small tea-plate. Round is a much more desirable shape today for packaging purposes, although the diehard who expects the oatcake to be triangular will be accommodated for some time yet. By yesteryear's standards our oatcakes are thin. Old cookery books refer to thick bannocks like the 'snoddie' and the 'mill bannock', the latter being twelve inches in diameter and an inch thick, with a hole in the middle; they certainly must have liked their oatcakes in those days!

In more superstitious times special properties were attributed to oatcakes. A large bannock placed above the door, for instance, was considered a protection against fairies taking away a newborn child, while the remedy for a cow cursed by a witch was to milk her through a hole made in a bannock.

The earliest method of baking oatcakes was to place the dough, made from meal and water, on a flat baking stone set at the side of the fire. A leap forward in technology, however, came with the introduction of the girdle. A girdle is a thin, round iron plate, with a semicircular handle attached to the sides in such a way that it may be suspended over a fire from a hook. The name is derived from the old French word *'gridil'*. The girdle was invented and first made in Culross, Fife. In 1599, James VI granted the burgh the exclusive privilege of manufacture and this was confirmed by Charles II in 1666. Later, a nearby ironworks took over its production. The girdle allowed quicker and more regular baking than was possible with the baking stone, although bannocks, after being lifted from the girdle, were often placed against a hot stone for a final hardening and toasting.

A variation of the girdle was the 'brander', where the flat surface was replaced by a series of wavy iron bars. The brander was used when the oatmeal was mixed with the meal from other crops such as beans, rye or barley when a stiffer dough was obtained.

Associated with the girdle was the scored or notched bannock stick for rolling out the meal mixture and, of course, the beautiful, heart-shaped instrument known by a variety of local names such as 'spathe' or 'spade', which was used to lift the hot oatcakes from the girdle. The girdle was never washed but would be cleaned when hot with coarse salt and a cloth or paper. It is interesting to note that spathes were seldom used in latter-day bakehouses because the bakery girls, eschewing the use of instruments, had become adept at lifting the baked oatcakes from large, hot iron plates with their fingers without suffering burns. Nowadays, of course, large-scale baking is not done on giant hot plates but in continuous ovens. But basic principles are the same. The mixing of the dough is still a slow, gentle process.

Nothing ever remains the same and no doubt there will be developments in oatcakes. What the manufacturers have up their sleeves is not known. Honey and cheese flavoured oatcakes have made their appearance, something I endorsed until inadvertently putting honey on a cheese flavoured oatcake one morning. As the prestigious 'Supermarket Magazine Award' in 1994 for the best bakery product went to Simmers for their cheese oatcake, it will surprise no one if other flavours appear on the market.

6
Haggis

Fair fa' your honest, sonsie face,
Great Chieftain o' the Puddin-race!
'To A Haggis', Robert Burns, 1787

He dwelt far up a Heelant glen
Where the foamin' flood and crag is,
He dined each day on the usquebae
An' he washed it doon wi' haggis.
'The Pawky Duke', David Rorie, 1867-1946

Alone amongst the oatmeal foods, haggis presents a caricature image. Stories of haggis-hunting abound (lie down beside it and make a noise like a precipice). It is difficult to see why the haggis should provoke such mirth. In every way it is a superb sausage, and if its skin should be a beast's paunch instead of its intestine (as encloses its Continental cousins), this merely emphasises the uniqueness of haggis.

The haggis has a proud history. The ancient Greeks as well as the Romans knew its pleasures; Dunbar mentions it in his fourteenth-century writings; Queen Victoria, in her diaries, records her enjoyment at eating haggis at Blair Castle during one of her journeys. No wonder Burns queried the right of anyone to regard it 'wi' sneerin', scornfu' view'.

The word 'haggis' seems to have been derived from the French *'hacher'* – to chop up or mangle. A French derivation would be appropriate for this old dish. Up to the time of the Union of the Crowns in 1603, French influence was strong in Scotland. In the days of the Auld Alliance, which after all dates back to 1295, commercial links between the two countries were close. French troops were stationed in Scotland, claret was the drink of the well-to-do, and it is not difficult to imagine some influence from that gastronomic land infiltrating Scottish kitchen habits. Indeed, there is proof that this did happen. In Scotland, a leg of lamb is invariably called a *'gigot'*, which is derived from an old French word for leg. A serving dish is an 'ashet' which almost certainly derives from the French 'assiette' for plate. There are many other examples and not only in the culinary field.

Burns, in his address 'To a Haggis', was not afraid to air his knowledge of French cuisine, even though it is obvious he thought but little of it:

Is there that owre his French ragout,
Or olio that wad staw a sow
Or fricassee wad mak her spew
Wi' perfect sconner,
Looks down wi' sneerin', scornfu' view
On sic a dinner?

After the collapse of the '45 rising, many Scots fled to France, taking their love of haggis with them. I am told it is still recognised in that food-conscious country today as *'Puding de St André'*, but I have to admit none of my French friends subscribe to this intelligence.

In terms of taste, haggis is supreme. It is only when some thought is given to its contents that an odd eyebrow may be raised. Yet heart and liver are good foods, and the oatmeal, onion and suet mixture has sustained the Scottish diet for ages with dishes like mealie puddings and skirlie-in-the-pan. There have been a few variations on the basic haggis mix. At one time a less coarse haggis was made of sheeps' tongues and kidneys and was well liked. Highland chiefs were reputed to banquet on haggis made with venison, while Haggis Royal contained mutton, vegetables and red wine. Isn't it high time some of our more enterprising manufacturers of meat products turned their attention to introducing new haggis lines based on these old recipes?

But always in haggis, oatmeal was and is a major ingredient; and, as has long been recognised, the best accompaniment to haggis is clapshot, a mixture of mashed potatoes and turnip with dripping and suet.

Burns' lines, in 'To a Haggis' ('Then, horn for horn, they stretch an' strive, De'il tak the hindmost, on they drive') remind us of the old custom of placing a bowl in the centre of the table for communal supping, when the youngsters, armed with long horn spoons, had to eat fast if their stomachs were not to remain empty. And today, as in Burns' time, haggis is a democratic dish, being enjoyed at all levels of society.

It is no longer common to see a sheep's pluck boiling in the kitchen (with the wind-pipe hanging over the side to let out the impurities), ready for the making of a haggis. But the steady guzzling of haggis, rising to a consumption peak at 'Burns' Supper' time, shows the Scots still think of haggis as a dish which stands 'abune them a'.' Currently in the United States there is a movement to introduce legislation which would abolish the sale of meat offal. Prohibition of achohol failed in that great country; could haggis prohibition succeed?

Akin to haggis is the white pudding. Well, white pudding if your loyalties are tied to the north, but a mealie pudding if your roots are in Edinburgh. If a Glaswegian, the comment is probably, 'I've heard of a black pudding, but what's a white pudding?'

The mealie/white pudding is a simple concoction of oatmeal, onions, suet, pepper and salt. In the archives of our national museums are old photographs showing crofters washing pigs' intestines at the water's edge in preparation for pudding making; so it seems reasonable to suggest the mealie/white pudding has a good bit of tradition behind it. Today's makers of puddings, of course, use a manufactured casing to hold the constituents together which, presumably, pleases the vegetarians and offends the back-to-nature lobby. But the pudding is not a standard item. In the north the demand is for lots of meal; as we move south it becomes more and more a fish and chip shop item to be cooked in deep fat and the suet and oatmeal balance changes. But all over the country the cut of oatmeal used is either coarse or pinhead. The amount of oatmeal used in black puddings is not significant.

7
Athole Brose

Leeze me on drink! it gie's us mair
Than either School or Colledge:
It kindles Wit, it waukens Lair,
It pangs us fou' o' Knowledge.
Be't whisky gill or penny wheep,
Or ony stronger potion,
It never fails, in drinkin deep,
To kittle up our notion,
By night or day.
'The Holy Fair', Robert Burns, 1786

Oatmeal does not readily suggest itself as the basis of an alcoholic drink. Athole Brose, though, is something different and has its following with many sophisticates throughout the world as the ideal drink with which to start a party. Doubtless the event will have a Scots overtone, although Athole Brose is no tartan gimmick; it is a drink which has stood the test of time.

The ingredients of Athole Brose are oatmeal, honey and whisky. For medicinal purposes an egg may be added and, with the growing custom of serving it as a sweet at the end of a meal, has come acceptance that cream may be included, although, in the opinion of the writer, this seems a funny way to treat a drink.

In her *Leaves from the Journal of our Life in the Highlands*, Queen Victoria records how she and Prince Albert drank

Athole Brose when they visited Blair Castle in the September of 1844. Many thousands of people visit that most beautiful castle at Blair Atholl every year, and it is a fair guess that most of them will indicate interest in the famous drink. Sir Henry Raeburn's famous painting of Niel Gow (1727-1807), our great fiddler and composer hangs in the castle ballroom. Gow, fiddler to four Dukes of Atholl, was, as the saying goes, fond of his dram. Walking home to Inver one early morning after playing at a castle function, Gow fell in with a crony who commiserated with him on the length of the road he had to travel. 'It's not the length of the road that worries me,' Gow is supposed to have said, 'It's the breadth.' On another occasion, on being asked by a passing acquaintance if he was getting home, he eloquently replied in the word, 'Whiles.' Agnes Lyon, wife of the minister at Glamis, acknowledging Gow's liking for drink, put words to Gow's tune, 'Farewell to Whisky'; particularly we remember the lines:

Aye since he wore the tartan trews,
He dearly lo'ed the Athole Brose.

While the origins of Athole Brose are obscure, its evolution can be understood. With the Highlanders' staple food of oatmeal and his own distilled spirit being carried during his travels, it is not difficult to imagine some simple experimentation with additives, and the cry of acclamation when honey was found to be the perfect partner to oatmeal and whisky.

There is, however, one legend which may explain how the drink came to be associated with the House of Athole. In the fifteenth century, Iain MacDonald, Earl of Ross and Lord of the Isles, was widely regarded as a dangerous menace to society and his capture was sought by many, including the Earl of Atholl. It came to the notice of Atholl that MacDonald frequently drank from a place where a hollow stone received water from a spring. The Earl gave instructions that the water should be diverted and the hollow stone filled with whisky and honey. In due course MacDonald came to the stone and, understandably, finding the water very much to his liking, dallied too long, becoming easy prey for Atholl's men.

Athole Brose gained a high reputation as a medicine. There is a story from the Atholl Estates, dated around 1800, of the daughter of an inhabitant of Atholl being placed in one of the first boarding schools in Edinburgh where she was seized with a violent fever. Her father was sent for as she was considered to be on the point of death. On his arrival he was told that everything the physicians could do for her had been done, but without effect. 'Has she had any Athole Brose?' he asked. On receiving a negative reply, he had a good dose of it instantly prepared and had the child swallow it and then happily watched her almost immediate recovery.

Robert Louis Stevenson seems to have been well acquainted with the drink which makes an appearance in his fiction:

> *Duncan Dhu made haste to bring out the pair of pipes*
> *that was his principal possession, and to set before his*
> *guests a mutton ham and a drink which they call Athole*
> *Brose, and which is made of old whisky, oatmeal,*
> *strained honey and sweet cream, slowly beaten together*
> *in the right order and proportion. Maclaren pressed them*
> *to taste his mutton-ham and the wife's brose, reminding*
> *them the wife was out of Athole and had a name far and*
> *wide for her skill in that confection.*

'Kidnapped', R. L. Stevenson, 1886

In his poem 'Athole Brose' though, Stevenson seems to have found a variation to the normal ingredients:

> *Willie and I cam doun by Blair*
> *And in by Tullibardine,*
> *The rye were at the waterside,*
> *An' bee-skeps in the garden.*
> *I saw the reek of a private still –*
> *Says I, 'Gud lord, I thank ye!'*
> *As Willie and I cam in by Blair*
> *And out by Killiecrankie.*

Ye hinny bees, ye smuggler lads,
Thou, Muse, the bard's protector,
I never kent what rye was for
Till I had drunk the nectar!
And shall I never drinkit mair?
Gud troth, I beg your pardon!
The neist time I cam doun by Blair
And in by Tullibardine.

Stevenson's reference to smugglers reminds us that millers were in a bartering position with smugglers, something David Webster would comment on in the early nineteenth century:

The smugglers whiles cam in wi' their packs,
'Cause they kent that I likit a bicker;
Sae I barter'd whiles wi' the gowks –
Gied them grain for a soup o' their liquor.
I had lang been accustom'd to drink:
And aye when I purposed to quat it,
The thing wi' its clapperty-clink
Said aye tae me, Tak it, man, tak it.

'Tak' it, Man, Tak it', David Webster, 1787-1837

While proprietary brands of Athole Brose are on the market, most regular users make up their own batches so as to produce a drink especially pleasing to their palate. The consumption of Athole Brose peaks at Burns' Supper time and St Andrew's Night and many a Scot returned from exile has regaled his friends with hair-raising stories about preparing quantities of the Brose with uncommon utensils in jungle or desert climes. Sir Robert Bruce Lockhart in his fine book, *Scotch* (1951), tells how he organised a St Andrew's dinner in the Czechoslovakian capital of Prague. Unfortunately he delegated the making of the Brose to a Sassenach who, in an attempt to make his mark, laced it with slivovice, the potent plum brandy. Sir Robert's comment that 'he suffered for his intervention in Scottish affairs' is, one can imagine, a masterpiece of understatement.

Boswell, in his *Life of Johnson*, shows that the great man's wisdom also extended into the topic of drinks:

> *Mr Eliot mentioned a curious liquor peculiar to his*
> *country, which the Cornish fishermen drink. They call*
> *it 'mahogany'; and it is made of two parts gin, and one*
> *part treacle, well beaten together. I begged to have*
> *some of it made, which was done with proper skill by*
> *Mr Eliot. I thought it very good liquor; and said it was*
> *a counterpart of what is called 'Athole Porridge' in the*
> *Highlands of Scotland, which is a mixture of whisky and*
> *honey. Johnson said, 'that must be a better liquor than*
> *the Cornish, for both its component parts are better.'*

'Life of Johnson', J. Boswell, 1791

As far as is known, Dr Johnson admired Athole Brose only from a distance. No record has been found of his having consumed it. But it is to be hoped that it was the sampling of the nectar that gave Thomas Hood's travelling friend the sparkle to his wit:

> *Charm'd with a drink which Highlanders compose,*
> *A German traveller exclaimed with glee, –*
> *'POTZTAUSEND! sare, if dis is Athole Brose,*
> *How goot der Athole Boetry must be!'*

Drinking stories abound in our Scottish literature and Atholl has its share. There is a delightful one about the old lady who had been prevailed upon to take the pledge. In due course she paid a visit to an old crony who was not aware of her reformed character. Athole Brose was produced and the lady was sorely tempted. But bravely she stuttered out, 'Nae thanks, I've promised never tae put ma hand or lips tae a glass again.' Then, as the bottle was being removed she added, 'If ye were tae put a wee drappie in a tea-cup I could maybe tak' it.'

8
Cream-crowdie or Crannachan

Ance crowdie, twice crowdie,
Three times crowdie in a day!
Gin ye crowdie ony mair,
Ye'll crowdie a' my meal away.
Song Quoted in Letter to Mrs Dunlop,
Robert Burns, 1793

The crowdie Burns was referring to in his lines differs considerably from the elegant sweet which today bears the Lowland, double-barrelled name of cream-crowdie or the Highland, Gaelic name of 'crannachan'. Burns was using the word 'crowdie' to indicate an oatmeal dish, in much the same way as in 'The Holy Fair', he uses the term 'crowdie-time' to indicate breakfast. The word, however, has a different meaning in other parts of the country. In the north-east, crowdie was the product of curds 'wrung' out in cheesecloth and left to hang and dry. In the Highlands, crowdie was a curds and butter combination and it is this mixture which has developed with the passing of time into the cream-crowdie or crannachan we so enjoy today.

As a mixture of toasted oatmeal, cream and sugar, crannachan was prepared for festive occasions, especially Hallowe'en, when small charms would be placed in it in much the same way that coins and trinkets are secreted in Christmas puddings today. Crannachan has always been a dish without a precise recipe, it being the custom for the lady of the house to make it according to her guidman's taste. This, we may take it, explains the addition of whisky, an incorporation we can trace back to 1787 when Andrew Shirreff wrote:

> *A cogie o' yill,*
> *An a pickle oatmeal,*
> *An' a dainty wee drappie o' whisky*
> *An' hey for the cogie*
> *An' hey for the yill –*
> *Gin ye steer a' thegither, they'll do unco weel.*
>
> 'A Cogie o' Till', Andrew Shirreff, 1787

But there was to be one further addition which would ensure its entry into gourmet circles.

The counties of Angus and Perthshire produce over eighty per cent of all the raspberries grown in Britain. The light loam encourages the free surface rooting necessary for the establishment and growth of healthy plants and the moist climate ensures plump and succulent berries. In this area, raspberry fields of many acres can be seen and there are   few country gardens without their row or two of rasps. With such a crop in superabundance, it was inevitable that housewives, besides making substantial quantities of jam, would find another use for their berries. Raspberries and cream have always been a popular treat in this area which is also renowned for the quality of its oats. The population is particularly sweet-toothed, a fact readily confirmed by the number of confectionery manufacturers who originated in the area and by the common practice of taking a dram with lemonade instead of water. The experiment of blending oatmeal, cream, whisky and raspberries is not difficult to imagine, and thus crannachan arrived on the scene as a sweet without equal.

The cottage-cheese seen on supermarket shelves is today's equivalent of crowdie and the healthy food fetish has seen it become a popular line. Frequently it contains an addition of herbs or even fruit. In the view of one man, the best way to enjoy this crowdie is to pile it on an oatcake spread with freshly salted butter. Then there is a royal feast of taste and texture.

9

A New Scene

> *And there will be lapper'd-milk kebbucks,*
> *And sowens, and farles, and baps,*
> *With swats, and well-scraped paunches,*
> *And brandy in stoups and in caps:*
> *And there will be mealkail and castocks*
> *And skink to sup till ye rive:*
> *And roasts to roast on a brander*
> *Of flowks that were taken alive.*
>
> Blythsome Bridal, Francis Sempill of Beltrees, 1616-1682

The word 'muesli' is of German-Swiss origin. I would not like to say the word or product was unknown to me when I first wrote the parent volume of this book. Nevertheless, I was not at first enchanted with the mealy mixture that was set before me at breakfast from time to time, even with the accompanying advice that it was a health food and would do me good. Porridge seemed a healthy enough meal. It took some time before I realised that oats were advancing on more than one front.

Oats for porridge consumption had gone into decline in the 1950s following the post-war years when many mills had modernised and increased their capacity. It is not an unfamiliar story. At an Oatmeal Millers' Convention held in Pitlochry in 1949, representatives from nearly two hundred mills in Scotland were present; at that time every locality could boast at least one oatmeal mill. Slowly at first, then with increasing acceleration, the mills were to close down, their numbers savaged. The few remaining diehards thankfully accepted the customers of their unlucky brethren.

It was not until the 1980s, and especially the latter part of the decade, that interest in oat foods revived with vigour. And that revival was due to the public's decision to make health foods fashionable. For years oats had been sold under the marketing banner of 'the hot breakfast that sets the individual on the right track for the day'. Now another route to the consumer's purse offered itself.

It was in America in the 1960s that the ability of oat products to reduce blood cholesterol was first noted; findings which were later confirmed in other countries. A leading dietary researcher, Dr James Anderson of Kentucky University, working with other researchers identified two different types of dietary fibre – water-insoluble and water-soluble. The insoluble fibre – wheat bran is a good example – provides us with roughage and bulk. But the soluble fibre, research has indicated, is useful in the prevention of coronary heart disease and in the treatment of some diabetic complaints. Oats and oat bran in particular are rich in soluble fibre, hence the interest shown in oats by researchers. A later study carried out at King's College, London and published in the *Journal of Clinical Nutrition and Gastroenterology* gave the finding that a low-fat diet and a daily intake of rolled oats had significantly reduced the blood cholesterol level of a group of volunteers.

As well as being a source of soluble and insoluble fibre, oats are rich in vitamins and contain more protein than most other grains. As interest in health foods increased, so did slimming clubs and those pursuing the latest weight-reducing fad started to count their calorie intake. Again, as with helping the body to break down cholesterol in the bloodstream, oats were to come out well, a porridge breakfast having less than half the calories of a bacon and egg one.

This was enough for the health enthusiasts; a surge of interest in porridge saw a smile appear on the millers' faces and consumption increased for the next few years without hindrance. But the porridge consumption was to get a boost from yet another source. The microwave became a commonplace piece of kitchen equipment around this time, receiving a warm welcome from working wives and husbands. Easy and quick to operate, it eliminated the need for messy pots. So, one of the practical (and perhaps psychological) barriers to the eating of porridge fell, because microwave porridge is good porridge and easily made, and a bowl from a microwave oven is easier to clean than a pot which has simmered on the cooker.

Aware that the health movement was set to last, manufacturers looked around for suitable foods to promote. Muesli, standing on the sidelines, met all the requirements. Already established in many European countries, attractive packaging and a health story would ensure its arrival on the supermarket shelves. One of the main constituents of muesli, frequently the major one, is flaked oats, and the Scottish oat growers and oatmeal millers again smiled. In fact the happy look stayed on their faces as, following some brilliant marketing work, leading biscuit manufacturers produced oat content biscuits with a taste to satisfy the palate of increasingly sophisticated consumers. Such biscuits today are bought in truly amazing quantities; the faith of the biscuit makers in oats has been justified.

But to return to muesli. Early mueslis were simple in the extreme. Flaked oats, raisins and sultanas, nuts and a little sweetening might have qualified as a health food some years ago. But nothing, or at least few things, remains the same. The public started to make a distinction between health foods and healthier eating. Those with their finger on the pulse realised muesli had to become more exciting, more appealing to discriminating palates while still projecting an aura of well-being. Other cereals found their way into the blend and the range of nuts was extended. Associated items such as wheat germ and sunflower seeds made their appearance. But most important of all was the decision to incorporate dried fruit. And for extra appeal the food manufacturers went, not only for the dried fruits of the consumer's normal usage but for exotic fruits from the tropics. Today an overwhelming range of mueslis is on offer.

Having learned how to introduce oats into more sophisticated company on grounds of taste, attention is now being given to improving eye appeal on the plate. There is no doubt the sight of a red chip of dried strawberry or green passion fruit adds brightness and attractiveness to a bowl of grains, but I reserve judgement on some of the new ideas being hatched out by our marketing specialists. Should we really be colouring our oat flakes a bright yellow and giving them a banana flavour? Will pineapple or blueberry flavoured porridge be more appealing to youngsters? Will the oat-chocolate combination be susceptible to overkill?

November 1994 saw the Government issue its 'Eat Your Way to Health' report which was to aim at reducing the number of deaths from heart disease and strokes, the most common killers in the country. It seems reasonable to suppose this report will encourage greater consumption of oat products. Once again Dr Johnson's definition of oats may appear in print —'a crop which sustains the Scots'.

10
Recipes

Scottish cooking is rich in recipes using oatmeal as a staple ingredient. In this small book it is only possible to give a small selection and I have chosen those which regularly grace my table and give pleasure to family and friends alike.

OATMEAL SOUP

An unusual, elegant and economical soup
for many occasions.

50g rolled oats
2 medium onions, chopped
1 large carrot, grated
2 tablespoons melted butter
1 pint chicken stock
1 pint milk
chopped parsley
salt and pepper
cream for garnishing (optional)

Melt butter in a large pan over low heat, add onions and carrot and cook gently for about 6 minutes; add oats to pan and cook for about 4 minutes, stirring frequently; add the stock little by little and season to taste; bring to the boil and simmer with lid on pan for 25–30 minutes; add parsley; add milk and heat through but do not boil; garnish with cream if desired.

(serves four to six)

ATHOLE BROSE
as an aperitif

Soak a quantity of pinhead oatmeal in water overnight; drain off the liquor and add honey to taste; add an equal amount of whisky. Pour into glasses to which a little oatmeal has been added.

ATHOLE BROSE
as a dessert

To a tablespoon of lightly toasted pinhead oatmeal add 1 tablespoon of honey and 2 tablespoons of whisky; mix well; gently fold this mixture into a pint of stiffly beaten cream.

CRANNACHAN

Surely this must be the most magnificent of all sweets!

75g pinhead oatmeal
½ pint double cream
1 tablespoon Drambuie
4 teaspoons honey
125g raspberries

Toast the oatmeal in a frying pan over a fairly high heat until it is lightly browned; sift out any dust; whisk the cream to a soft consistency; mix in the Drambuie and honey; combine with raspberries; sprinkle a little roasted oatmeal on top if desired.

(Serves four)

BROONIE

This recipe is reputed to have originated in Orkney. It is high time it was introduced into those windswept isles.

125g plain flour
125g flaked oats
150g dark brown sugar
6 tablespoons treacle
100g butter
½ teaspoon salt
3 teaspoons ground ginger
2 teaspoons baking powder
1 egg
½ pint milk

Heat treacle, sugar and butter over a low heat until butter is melted; mix sieved flour, baking powder, ginger, salt and flaked oats in a large bowl; beat egg in a separate bowl; add milk to beaten egg; add egg and milk mixture to treacle mixture; add the resultant mixture gradually to the flour mixture and mix thoroughly; then (if you are not by that time too mixed up!). Place mixture in a loaf tin and bake in a moderate oven (180°C, Gas Mark 4) for about an hour.

MUESLI

The make-up of one's own muesli is a very personal thing.
In the first edition of this book I gave the following recipe:

200g flaked oats
50g raisins
50g sultanas
25g soft brown sugar
25g chopped peanuts

Well, muesli has moved on quite a bit since those days, so
add as your palate dictates, not forgetting chopped dried
fruits, an extended range of nuts and a touch of bran and
wheatgerm. Mix well and rely on plain or flavoured yoghurt
for your moisture.

SKIRLIE

'A mealie pudding without the skin', it is said. Not strictly
accurate but not a bad description. Excellent with a wide
range of main dishes.

50g butter or roast beef dripping
1 finely chopped onion
flaked oats or coarse oatmeal according to preference
freshly-ground black pepper
salt

Melt butter or dripping over medium heat and add onion.
Stir until onion is lightly browned; add oats slowly until all
fat is absorbed and the mixture fairly firm; add seasoning
and keep stirring for about eight minutes.

OATMEAL STUFFING

A very traditional stuffing for poultry or game.

200g flaked oats
1 onion finely chopped
100g shredded suet
seasoning

Mix all ingredients in a bowl and stuff poultry or game in the usual way.

HERRING IN OATMEAL

filleted herring
seasoning
oatmeal
lard or dripping

Season the fillets and toss in oats until thoroughly covered; fry in hot fat, turning occasionally, for about seven minutes; serve with a mustard sauce.

OATCAKES

400g oatmeal
50g butter
1 cup boiling water
a pinch of baking soda
a pinch of salt

Mix all ingredients together and roll out thin; cut into rounds and bake in a moderate oven until crisp. (Alternatively, use a girdle if you are lucky enough to have one. The hotplate of a Rayburn or an Aga is a good substitute.)

SWEET BANNOCKS

175g flaked oats
100g self-raising flour
50g lard
25g margarine
100g sugar
4 tablespoons water

Combine oatmeal, flour and sugar in a bowl; melt lard and margarine with four tablespoons of water in a pan and pour on the oat, flour and sugar mixture; mix well, roll out and cut into shapes: place on a baking tray and bake for 15 minutes at 200°C (Gas Mark 6); turn oven down to a minimum heat and leave for a further ten minutes.

MEALIE CANDY

1½ kilos sugar
400g treacle
200g toasted oatmeal
50g ground ginger
1¼ pints water

Put sugar, treacle and 1¼ pints of water in a pan and bring to the boil; boil for ten minutes; remove pan from heat; with a wooden spoon, rub the syrup gently against the side of the pan until creamy; stir in the oatmeal and ginger; pour the mixture into tins lined with oiled paper and cut into pieces when cool.

BLENSHAW
(*Blanche Eau*)

I was delighted to hear recently that some farmworkers were still using this as a harvest drink.

oatmeal

sugar

milk

water

nutmeg

Put a teaspoon of oatmeal into a tumbler with the same amount of sugar; pour in half a gill of milk and stir until creamy; pour on boiling water to fill glass; grate some nutmeg over the mixture and drink when cool. I have often wondered about the origins of this old drink.

11

The Poetry and Prose of Oats

Scottish literature is full of references to oatmeal and its many uses and benefits. While researching for this book, I have come across many which deserve notice but do not fit into the body of the book. Rather than lose them, I have put them into this separate section.

Till eke their cheer ane subcharge furth sho brocht,
Ane plate of groatis,and ane dish full of meal;
Thraf cakis als I trow sho sparit nocht,
Abundantly about her for to deal.
'The Taill of the Uponlandis Mous', Robert Henryson, *c.*1420-1490

Queen Victoria's *Highlands Journals* note:

September 11 — Wednesday 1844
We passed the point of Logierait, where are the remains
of an ancient castle – the old Regality Court of the
Dukes of Athole. At Moulinearn we tasted some of the
Athole Brose, which was brought to the carriage.

October 13 – Thursday 1865
The Duchess has a very good cook, a Scotchwoman,
and I thought how dear Albert would have liked it all.
He always said things tasted better in smaller houses.
There were several Scotch dishes, two soups, and the
celebrated 'haggis', which I tried last night, and really
liked very much. The Duchess was delighted at my
taking it.

Perhaps the good Queen had read Fergusson's poem, 'A Drink Eclogue', about the contents of a haggis and for once was amused:

Imprimis, then a haggis fat,
Weel tottled in a seethin' pat,
Wi' spice and ingans weel ca'ed through,
Had help'd to gust the stirrah's mou',
And placed itsel' in truncher clean
Before the gilpy's glowrin' een.

But it was Dr Johnson's definition of oats that really riled Fergusson; his sarcasm knew no bounds:

Welcome, thou verbal potentate and prince!
To hills and valleys, where emerging oats
From earth assuage our pauperty to bay,
And bless thy name, thy dictionaire skill,
Which there definitive will still remain,
And oft be speculized by taper blue,
While youth studentious turn thy folio page.

To be fair to Fergusson though, he may ultimately have forgiven Johnson as the Southron eventually passed some kind remarks about our fare:

Let Wilkes and Churchill rage no more,
Tho' scarce provision, learning's good:
What can these hungries next explore?
Even Samuel Johnson loves our food.
        'Preamble to Dr Samual Johnson',
        Robert Fergusson, 1750-1774

Allan Ramsay, too, thought the food of old Scotland worthy of a mention in rhyme:

For here yestreen I brewed a bow of maut,
Yestreen I slew twa wethers prime and fat.
A furlet of good cakes, my Elspa beuk,
And a large ham hangs reesting in the neuk.
I saw mysel', or I cam o'er the loan,
Our muckle pot that scads the whey, put on,

A mutton-bouk to boil, and ane we'll roast;
And on the haggies Elspa spares nae cost.
Small are they shorn, and she can mix fu' nice
The gusty ingans wi' a curn of spice;
Fat are the puddings, – heads and feet weel sung.

'The Gentle Shepherd', Allan Ramsay, 1682-1758

And even a hundred years earlier than Allan Ramsay, one of the Sempills of Beltrees in 'The Blythesome Bridal' would confirm the Scots table could groan under simple fare presented in a variety of ways:

There'll be tartan, dragen, and brochan,
And fouth o' guid gabbocks o' skate,
Powsowdie, and drammock, and crowdie,
And caller nowt-feet on a plate.
And ther'll be partans and buckies,
And speldins and haddocks enew,
And singit sheep heads and a haggis,
And scadlips to sup till ye're fou.

Despite his un-Scottish sounding name, Tobias Smollett was born on the north side of the border. Here in *Humphrey Clinker* he takes a somewhat outside view of his native land's foods:

Now we are upon the article of cookery, I must own,
some of their dishes are savoury, and even delicate; but
I am not yet Scotchman enough to relish their singed
sheep's head and haggis, which were provided, at our
request, one day at Mr. Mitchelson's, where we dined.
The first put me in mind of the history of Congo, in
which I had read of negroes' heads sold publicly in the
markets; the last, being a mess of minced lights, livers,
suet, oatmeal, onions, and pepper, enclosed in a sheep's
stomach, had a very sudden effect upon mine, and the
delicate Mrs. Tabby changed colour; when the cause of
our disgust was instantly removed at the nod of our
entertainer. The Scotch in general are attached to this
composition with a sort of national fondness, as well as

*to their oatmeal bread; which is presented at every table,
in thin triangular cakes, baked upon a plate of iron,
called a girdle; and these many of the natives, even in the
higher ranks of life, prefer to wheaten bread, which they
have here in perfection.*
'The Expedition of Humphrey Clinker', Tobias Smollett, 1771

Amongst the farming poetry of our land, Charles Murray's
'Hint O' Hairst' must be regarded as one of the most com-
pelling and authentic poems to come from the north-east:

*O for a day at the Hint o' Hairst,
With the craps weel in an' stackit,
When the farmer steps thro' the corn-yard,
An' counts a' the rucks he's thackit.*

*When the smith stirs up his fire again,
To sharpen the ploughman's coulter;
When the miller sets a new picked stane,
An' dreams o' a muckle moulter.*

*When cottars' kail get a touch o' frost,
That mak's them but taste the better;
An' thro' the neeps strides the leggined laird,
Wi's gun an' a draggled setter.*

*When the forester wi' axe an' keel
Is markin' the wind-blawn timmer,
An' there's truffs aneuch at the barn gale
To reist a' the fires till simmer.*

*Syne o for a nicht, ae lang forenicht,
Ower the dambrod spent or cairtin',
Or keepin' tryst wi' a neebour's lass –
An' a mou held up at pairtin'.*

Another poet from the north-east, but one who portrayed a
greater sense of humour than Murray, was George Abel, a
country minister. Here in 'The Meal and Ale' from his book,
Wylins Fae My Wallet (1916) is true Doric delight:

They planned it at the market, far they baith were buying
    kye,
Wi' a sample o' the barley i' their queyt,
That Blackie till his meal and ale wad tak' a step ower by,
An' like neepours hae a hamely sup and bite.

'But min,' said Mains, 'the ploitery roads, an' that the
    mee'ns awa';
Ye'll be seer to fesh a lantern i' your hand:
Your een are no sae clever as when we were laddies twa,
Gin ye snapper at the briggie ye'll be pranned.'

So Blackie took his lantern - fin the wife had made him
    snod –
An' got throwe the clorty feedles wintin' hairm,
He sowfed himsel' across the brig, an' up the Tinklers'
    Road,
Then he lap the style 'at stan's forenent the fairm.

The nicht went by like winkin' – Och I min' the splorey
    weel –
But the fairmers didna fash the kitchie lang;
They slippit ben the hoose, far ale was rifer than the meal,
An' they blebbet there till baith their heids were wrang.

'Twas twal fin Blackie startit fir his biggin' yont the burn,
But he feared na fire nor water, man nor deil,
Lat him only get his lantern 'at had deen sae weel its turn,
An' he'd cairry Main's ale as easy's meal.

He ne'er gied a' the rinnins i' the hameward tramp that
    nicht,
But he thocht he beddit's lantern at the stack.
He swore 'twas byous wechty, an' most awfu' scrimp o'
    licht,
An' whene'er he spak he aye got answer back.

His mistress tell't me froonin', o' the proticks o' her man,
An' that Mains sent owre a letter in a rage;
'Dear Sir, – Herewith's your lantern, at' ye left upo' my han',
You will please return my parrot an' my cage.'

A somewhat different Meal and Ale is recounted by James Thomson. Robin and his helper are struggling to finish their rig on kirn-day when disaster strikes:

We cleared our rig baith tight and clean,
And thought the day our ain,
When wae's my heart! I brak' my huik
Upon a meikle stane.
'Mak bands,' quo Robin – while the sweat
Like rain-drops trickled doon; –
But Robin reach'd the land-end first
And foremost o' the boon.

I thought that I wad swoon wi' joy
When dightin' Robin's brow,
He says, 'Meg, gin ye'll buckle to,
I'll shear through life wi' you.'
What could I do but buckle to -
He was sae frank and free?
And often did I bless the day
That Robin shuire wi' me.

'Hairst', James Thomson of Hawick, 1827-1888

Oatmeal millers in the past had a reputation for wealth, as it was said: 'There iss men that iss oatmeal millers – and there iss men that hass a puckle money.'

As far back as the first part of the eighteenth century, Sir John Clerk of Penicuik could write:

When Jamie first did woo me,
I speir'd what was his calling:
'Fair maid', says he, 'O come and see,
Ye're welcome to my dwelling'.
Though I was shy, yet I could spy
The truth of what he told me
And that his house was warm and couth,
And room in it to hold me.

Behind the door a bag of meal;
And in his kist was plenty
Of good hard cakes his mither bakes,
And bannocks werena scanty:
A good fat sow; a sleeky cow
Was standin' in the byre;
While lazy puss, wi' mealy mou',
Was playing at the fire.

Wealth of course frequently leads to drink, but as Charles Murray points out, there can be other reasons for drinking:

Week in an' week oot, when I'm millin',
The sids seem to stick in my throat;
Nae wonder at markets I'm willin
To spend wi' a crony a groat.
An' if I've a shaltie to niffer,
Or't maybe some barley to sell,
An oonslockened bargain's aye stiffer —
Ye ken that fu' brawly yersel'.
Fae forebears my thirst I inherit,
As others get red hair or gout;
The heirship's expensive: nae merit
To me that I never cry out.
An' sae, man, I canna help thinkin'
The neighbours unkindly; in truth,
Afore they can judge o' my drinkin'
They first maun consider my drooth.
'The Miller Explains', Charles Murray, 1864-1941

And if the demon drink wasn't enough to contend with, the miller had to remember many a girl saw him as a desirable husband:

When I gaed to the mill my lane,
For to grind my malt,
The miller-laddie kissed me;
I thought it was nae fau't.
What though the laddie kissed me,
When I was at the mill!

73

A kiss is but a touch;
And a touch can do no ill.

O I loo the miller-laddie!
And my laddie lues me;
He has sic a blyth look,
And a bonnie blinking ee.
What though the laddie kissed me,
When I was at the mill!
A kiss is but a touch;
And a touch can do no ill.

From 'Scottish Songs', David Herd, 1869

Glossary

A', all
ABUNE, above
AITS, oats
ANCE, once
ANE, one
AULD, old

BAGGIE, the belly, stomach
BAPS, rolls
BAUDRONS, cat, pussy
BEN, through
BEUK, bake
BIGGIN, house, building
BIN'IN, binding
BLINTERIN, unseeing
BLYTHER, more cheerful
BOW, boll, a measure of
   140 lbs
BOWIE, a milk pail, a dish
BRIGGIE, a bridge
BROCHAN, an oatmeal
   preparation
BUCKIE, a winkle
BYOUS, not common

CA'D, driven
CANTILT, cheerily
CASTOCKS, stalk of kail or
   cabbage
CAUP, vessel or bowl
CLAW, scratch of head
   indicating astonishment
CLORTY, dirty
COG, bowl
CRAIG, throat
CRATER, creature, whisky
CRONACH, lament
CROWDIE, a cream cheese
CROWDIE, an oatmeal dish

DIGHT, clean, wipe
DOON, down
DOUGHTY, valiant
DOWIE, sad, weak
DRAFF, wet barley husks
DRAGEN, an oatmeal
   preparation
DRAMMOCK, oatmeal and
   cold water

DRIBBLES, succession of drops, gentle flow of water

DWALT, dwelt

EEN, eyes

EKE, to join, increase

ENEUCH/ENEW, enough

FAIR FA', welcome,

FALLOW, fellow

FARL, oatcake baked on one side

FASH, trouble

FESH, fetch

FIN, when

FORENENT, over against

FOWK, folk

FRICASS, minced meat in gravy

FU', full

FURLOT, firlot, quarter of a boll

GAB, the mouth, to speak pertly

GAR, make

GABBOCKS, mouthfuls

GAE'D SKELPIN' BEN, raced into next room

GANG, to go

GAUCY, plump

GEAR, riches, goods of any kind

GIED, gave

GIF, if, whether

GILPY, a girl

GIN, if, before, until

GLOWERIN', staring angrily

GOWK, cuckoo, fool

GROAT, silver coin valued at around four old pence, kernel of an oat

GROATIS, groats

GUST, to taste

HAMEIL, domestic, homely

HEELANT, Highland

HEID, head

IMPRIMIS, firstly

INGAN, onion

JURRAM, song, lullaby

KEBBOCK, cheese (especially home made)

KIST, storage chest

KITCHIE, kitchen

KITTLE, tickle, stir

KYE, cattle

LAP, leap, spring

LAPPER, ripple

LAPPIE, small pool of water, puddle

LEAR, teach

LEEZE ME, I'm fond of

LOAN, lane, farm road

MAIR, more

MAUT, malt

MEEN, moon

MILL E'E, the mill eye, the opening in the top of a grinding stone

MINNEER, great noise

76

MOU', mouth

MOULTER, mulcture (payment to a mill owner)

MUCKLE, much, large

MUTTON-BOUK, whole carcass of a sheep

NA, no

NAE, no

NEUK, nook, corner

NIFFER, bargain, haggle

NOWT-FEET, dish of cow-heels

OLIO, a stew

ON THE BENT, in the open

ONY, any

OONSLOCKENED, drink, (usually to seal a deal)

OWRE, over

PANG, pack tight, cram

PARTAN, crab

PAT, pot

PEERIE, spinning top, object shaped like a spinning top

PEERIE, small, little

PICKLE, a small quantity

PLOITER, to work aimlessly

PLOITERY, wet, muddy

PRANNED, to hurt, crush

PROTICK, an adventure

QUAIET, quiet

QUEYT, coat

RAGOUT, well spiced meat

RAX, to stretch

REAM, to foam, to cream

REEK, smoke

REET, the bottom, the foot

RINNINS, main outlines

SCAD, scald

SCADLIPS, a thin barley broth

SCONNER, disgust

SHAVE-SHAVER, a funny fellow

SHUIRE, sure

SEER, sure

SHALTIE, pony

SIC, SICKEN, such

SIDS, dust from husks

SNAPPER, stumble

SNOD, tidy, neat

SONSIE, pleasant, homely

SOUPLE, flexible, swift

SOWANS, extract from steeped husks and meal

SOWF, a low whistle

SPELDINS, split, dried fish

SPEW, to vomit

SPLORE, frolic

STAW, surfeit

STEEVE, firm

STIRRAH, a young man

STRAE, straw

STOUP, carrying or drinking vessel

SUBCHARGE, something additional, a second dish or course

SWATS, weak beer

TAE, to

TARTAN, meal and cabbage dish

TENT, to heed

THRAF, unleavened

TRUNCHER, a trencher or platter

TWA, two

TWAL, twelve

WAD, would

WAUKENS, wakens

WAME, womb or belly

WASHT, tired

WECHT, sieve-like tool for winnowing corn, a weight

WEEL, well

WETHER, a castrated ram

WHEEP, whistle, or a shrill cry

WI', with

WINTIN, without

YESTREEN, yesterday

YILL, ale

YOKIN, working period

YONT, beyond, apart